ALL ABOUT PADEL

ALL ABOUT PADEL

THE COMPLETE GUIDE FOR BEGINNERS

KIM FELDMANN

OPPIAN

Published by Oppian Press

Helsinki, Finland

ISBN 978-951-877-781-9

CONTENTS

AMONG THE GENEALOGY of all sports, Padel (from Spanish pádel meaning paddle) belongs to the family of "racquet sports". And like any racquet sport, it is a direct descendant of tennis. As such, padel embodies its predecessor's rules and regulations, its tactical mentality, its jargon and etiquette. Both practices essentially follow the same objective: to use the racquet, or paddle, to hit a ball over the net and onto the opponent's side, attempting to make it bounce twice to avoid committing a fault. Even the scoring takes the same 15s, game, set, match format. These similarities corroborate why padel is often seen as a version of tennis, but one might also call it a cross-pollination between tennis and squash, since it boasts the latter's fast pace and dynamism. Still, padel has idiosyncrasies that distinguish it from its close siblings and render it a sport of its own.

Anyone watching or playing a match of padel will notice its main distinguishing feature straight away. Instead of serving above-head – one of the most physically and technically restrictive moves in conventional tennis – padel players serve underarm, bouncing the ball and hitting it below the waistline. This aspect alone makes for a less intense start, allowing the opponent to easily return the serve and the point to carry on. This means that almost anyone, regardless of technical know-how, can begin playing at once. The stringless racquet – or paddle – used by padel players is shorter and lighter than a tennis racquet and has a solid, perforated surface. The ball is akin to that of tennis, only slightly depressurised. With this more elementary equipment, players needn't apply powerful strokes to get the ball over the net, making it an overall less strenuous practice ideal for all physical conditions.

Likewise influencing the facility of play is the layout of the pitch. As in squash, a match of padel takes place on an enclosed court, and shots can be hit off the (usually glass) walls. An extra dimension makes the game more dynamic, with the average rally lasting between 10-15s, compared to 3-

5s in tennis. The playing area is roughly a third of the size of conventional tennis. Single-format games, carried out on a 6×20m court, aren't unheard of. Yet, padel is mostly a doubles game played in pitches of 10×20m. Such a significantly smaller area means players need to cover less ground during the point, therefore avoiding the explosive moves and short-distance dashes ever-present in tennis. Being closer together also encourages social interaction – an integral quality in padel – rendering the sport popular for its cooperative and strategic inclinations.

"If tennis is checkers, padel is chess," says Lee Sponaugle, President of All Racquet Sports USA, the country's leading padel-related institution. What Sponaugle refers to is one of the subtle, underlying differences between tennis and padel. The first draws largely on the player's expertise to finish off the point. The latter draws on the player's ability to keep the ball at play until the point finishes. Or, as the professional player and tournament director, Kendall Osbourne, puts it, "[At padel] you should never drive the ball with the intention of ending the point. Use the drive only to set yourself up for a better opportunity." Incidentally, this strategic tendency makes padel less reliant on strength and power and more on vision and cooperation between partners.

Partnership, cooperation, and inclusiveness are indeed the main factors responsible for attracting so many players. Padel is often regarded as a family sport, popular among male and female, youth and senior. It invites everyone to play together without skill level and physical strength making or breaking the match. American pro John Milbank describes padel as "A game of will [rather] than skill." He remarks that the sport is "More about the mental aspect of competition than it is about the talent/physical aspects," and that "You don't need to be a young, great athlete to excel at the game."

Beyond being inclusive, padel is a great aerobic exercise. Several studies have been conducted to assess its benefits on improving overall fitness, as well as coordination and reflexes in different age and gender groups. Psychologically, the sport stimulates goal-setting and paced evolution, both of which foster a personal commitment to achieving your best and knowing your limits. Teamwork is a cardinal part of padel, and when observed collectively, the dynamics involved in succeeding in a match hone intrapersonal and interpersonal values to be carried outside the court. Whether playing with family members, co-workers, friends, or strangers, the level of co-dependence in actions and responsibilities allows for unique types of bonding, all of which is compounded by the sheer fun and active lifestyle the game promotes.

Though often associated with platform tennis or paddle tennis (aka Pop Tennis) to the point of being used inter-changeably, padel is a sport of its own. Firstly, it is unique because of fundamental elements such as a walled perimeter around the court and the use of an actual tennis ball as opposed to a soft sponge rubber. Secondly, and perhaps most importantly, unlike its American counterparts, the Mexican origin of padel bore particular motifs, directing its evolution toward a distinct track which, despite their shared heritage, led to independent governing bodies.

Padel has currently about 18 million active players in more than 54 countries, out of which 300 thousand are part of one of the 43 national federations. Padel is the second-most-popular sport in Spain, with around 6 million players and 20 thousand courts. It has been considered one of the fastest-growing sports in the world, with names like footballer Lionel Messi, British tennis professional Jamie Murray, and Liverpool F.C. manager Jurgen Klopp as avid advocates. Though not yet an Olympic sport, the International Padel Federation has a development programme in place to expand the sport and meet the eligibility threshold. One thing is certain, however: it may have taken longer than tennis to popularise, but padel is here to stay.

AS A BY-PRODUCT of other racquet sports, the history of padel is somewhat hazy. Although documents and literature confirm that the current version of the sport is less than a hundred years old, it wouldn't be far-fetched to say that its history began in the 12th century. It surely makes sense to relate the origin of padel to that of tennis, whose modern edition (officially known as "lawn tennis") became popularised in the late 19th century in England. Likewise, it wouldn't be unfair to affirm that its inception branched off from the two American inventions of similar name and rules created in New York in the 20th century, which remain its closest siblings.

FROM HAND TO RACQUET TO PADDLE

Back in the 1200s, the Jeu de paume ("game of the palm" or "palm game") set forth a novel branch of ball-and-court games. It began in northern France and was soon introduced to Paris by Louis X, where it picked up momentum. The game had its own set of rules and regulations, with at least three players on each side whose objective was to strike the ball with the palm of the hand over a net and onto the other side of the court. It was played both outdoors (as longue paume or "long palm") and indoors (as courte paume or "short palm").

The game spread across Europe, and in the 16th century, the first racquets were introduced. Around the same time, "Jeu de paume" metamorphosed into "tennis". The name was adapted from the French tenez ("take" in English), which players commonly called out to their opponents before serving. Tennis underwent a boom in Britain, where it was played mainly on enclosed, indoor courts, with the possibility of hitting the ball off the walls – thus bearing the first vestiges of contemporary padel. It eventually became known as real tennis or royal tennis.

New iterations of the game emerged in the following

years, including the one referred to as lawn tennis, believed to have been instigated by the invention of the lawnmower in 1830, in England. Sources point to this early version of padel as a popular pastime among sailors and passengers of British ships during the 19th century, who made use of paddles to hit the ball, also utilising the walls in the game.

Toward the end of the 1800s, tennis courts suffered a transformation that would incite the development of what was to be a sport less like tennis and more like padel. Intending to teach children how to play, Michigan-based reverend Frank Beal made a few alterations to the game. He redesigned the dimensions of a tennis court to half of its original size, switched tennis balls for rubber balls, and opted for a solid wooden paddle instead of a racquet. After gaining popularity in Michigan, the new sport travelled with Beal when he relocated to Manhattan. There, it disseminated to the public at large, in particular to less privileged and more crowded areas whose populations couldn't access real tennis courts.

Prompted by Beal's project, the municipality started to build several Paddle Tennis courts in and around New York. The first official Paddle Tennis tournament took place in 1922, and in a few years, the United States Paddle Tennis Association (USPTA) was set up. Paddle Tennis soon became one of the country's most popular recreational activities; over 500 US cities adopted the practice, and some educational institutions adopted it as a part of their P.E. programme.

Meanwhile, in 1928, in Scarsdale, New York, Fessenden Blanchard and James Cogswell made a few changes to paddle tennis. Their main goal was for those who couldn't benefit from the cover of tennis clubs to be able to play throughout winter. Blanchard and Cogswell devised a mobile wooden platform that was placed a few centimetres above ground, making it easy to clear the court and thus play outdoors even after heavy snowfall – hence the name "platform tennis". Later, the duo also surrounded the pitch with taut chicken wire fences. First, this was done in order to prevent the balls from leaving the field. But soon the walls became part of the game, and players were allowed to hit the ball off the fence.

Like paddle tennis, platform tennis was usually played in doubles, with a spongy ball and a perforated paddle. After a relatively unsuccessful beginning, this new sport underwent a few modifications, eventually becoming a popular autumn and winter alternative to tennis in states like Washington D.C., New Jersey, and New York.

FROM PADDLE TO PADEL

When regarding padel for the distinct sport it has become (after all, platform tennis and pop tennis have independent governing bodies) and considering the official account by the International Padel Federation, its ontology begins in 1969, in Mexico. And like any good creation, the birth of padel was sprinkled with fortuity.

Mexican businessman Enrique Corcuera adapted an existing fronton court at his holiday home in Puerto de Acapulco by adding another wall on the opposite end, two smaller sidewalls, and a net at the centre. At first, he had conceived this setup at his home in Jalisco as a means to stop the ball from going into the neighbour's property during matches of Basque pelota. But after trying out the new court, he realised it could be used and developed into something else.

As per the first rulebook presented to Corcuera by his wife, defence players could hit the ball after it bounced off the walls, provided it had touched the ground beforehand. Corcuera borrowed both the ball and the scoring of tennis. The racquets were the same short, stringless paddles used in the US for platform tennis. He called the new game "Paddle Corcuera" and thus began the history of what we know today as padel.

After his 1974 summer holiday in Acapulco, one of Corcuera's friends, the Spanish businessman Alfonso de Hohenlohe, brought the sport to Spain. He redesigned the court slightly, namely by substituting the side walls with wire mesh fences, and modified the rules to make the sport more competitive. The first two courts were built at the Marbella Club, a hotel owned by de Hohenlohe, and the news about the sport disseminated among club members, including famous figures like Spaniard tennis player Manolo Santana. Soon, padel spread around Costa del Sol and across Spain, with Club Puerta de Hierro acquiring the first five courts in Madrid and the suburb of La Moraleja becoming a hub of the sport.

Like many tourists to the Marbella, Argentine millionaire Julio Menditeguy was instantly hooked when introduced to padel. With the help of fellow Argentinian businessmen, he imported the practice to his home country in 1969, where the first courts were built in Mar del Plata and Buenos Aires. Padel took off in Menditeguy's country within a few years, growing from dozens to hundreds of courts and thousands of players and becoming the second-most practised sport in Argentina after football. In 1987, the world's first official padel governing body – the Asociacion Platense de Padel (APPTAS) – was created. It was followed by the Argentinian Paddle Association (APA) a year later, with Menditeguy as part of the directive commission.

Spain only experienced an explosive effect akin to Argentina toward the end of the 90s, when, nudged by famous figures in politics and business, as well as the sports media, its number of players and courts grew exponentially. Nonetheless, in the wake of the Argentine administrative initiative, Concha Galatas, Pedro Ballvé, and Rafael Silvela joined forces to form the Spanish Padel Association in 1987. Much like its South American equivalent, the association aimed to organise and promote the development of padel in the country, expanding it to other regions of Spain like Barcelona, the Basque Country.

Throughout the 80s, padel was seen not only as a sport, but also as a business opportunity, and received extensive support from institutions both in Spain and Argentina. This was mainly because it was a highly inclusive sport, welcoming children, the elderly, women, the physically disabled, and families alike. Besides being a social game that was fun to watch, padel also promoted a healthy lifestyle, increasingly stirring interest in other countries. In the Americas, it spread to Chile, Uruguay, Brazil, Canada, and the United States. In Europe, courts began to pop up in France and Italy.

A significant turning point in the international dissemination of padel took place in 1989 in Argentina. Coach Jorge Galeotti designed what he called the "Crystal Palace", a mobile glass padel court that could easily be transported anywhere and mounted in both indoor or outdoor facilities. The invention was met with huge success in Mar del Plata and kickstarted a new age for the sport, as viewers now had a full perspective of the match.

With the turn of the decade, Padel began to deepen its roots. Following talks between Argentinian, Spanish, and Uruguayan associations, the Federacion Internacional de Padel (FIP) was established in Madrid in 1991. Spaniard Julio Alegria Artiach, the first president, directed the board responsible for drafting competition regulations and setting up an international circuit. The FIP hosted the first World Padel Championship, held in 1992 in Madrid, with the Crystal Palace having its European debut at the finals in Seville. Participants from Argentina, France, Spain, Italy, Uruguay, England, Mexico, and Paraguay formed the national teams. Argentina claimed the title over Spain in both the men's and women's category.

The year 1993 marked another turning point for padel both in Spain and the world. Besides being introduced to the USA and welcoming the US Padel Association, padel was acknowledged as an official sport by the High Council for Sports of Spain. The status spurred the creation of the Federacion Espanola de Padel (Spanish Padel Federation) in 1997, and the institution took charge of regulating the sport on a national level. Among the many changes implemented was the formalisation of the name as "padel", instead of "paddle", as it was known in Argentina.

Hoping to further unify Argentinian and Spanish practices, the federation also addressed matters related to rules and court features. Volleying the return in serve-and-volley moves, for example, which wasn't allowed in Argentina, became a legitimate part of the rulebook. Where courts in Argentina usually had side walls measuring 1.4 metres in height, the standard 3-metre-high, perimetric wire fence in Spanish courts was set as the norm. And even though the synthetic turf found in Spanish courts rendered the game much slower than Argentina's concrete surfaces, the new regulation stipulated that all surface types (natural/artificial, concrete, parquet, clay, or synthetic) remained valid. It ruled the same for the equipment used by players.

In 1994, Argentina hosted the second World Padel Championship in Mendoza. This time, twelve national teams attended the contest (Spain, Argentina, France, Mexico, England, Paraguay, Italy, Uruguay, Canada, Brazil, Chile, and the US) and Argentina once more won both categories. Subsequent World Championships were held in Mexico, France, and Canada, among other countries, and nations like Portugal, Sweden, Belgium, Austria, and Switzerland soon joined. These contests contributed to the speedy worldwide propagation of padel, consequently consolidating its position as an international sport.

MODERN TIMES

After the turn of the century, countries like the UK, Portugal, Russia, and Finland set up their independent federations. While France began building more courts in Toulouse, Florida welcomed some of the United States' first public padel courts, and clubs were established in Miami and Los Angeles. Meanwhile, Spain boasted over 500 padel clubs, with hotels nationwide joining the trend.

In 2005, the Association of Professional Players of Padel (AJPP) and the Spanish Feminine Association of Padel (AFEP) teamed up with tournament organisers to form the first professional circuit – the Padel Pro Tour. The tour had a male and female ranking and an official season calendar that took the world's elite players to compete in Spain and Argentina. The Padel Pro Tour was discontinued in 2012 and replaced by the World Padel Tour (WPT) in 2013. The new format, similar to tennis' ATP and WTA, started in Spain and travelled to Monaco, Andorra, Portugal, Argentina, and Dubai. At present, between 15-20 tournaments take place every year, as well as a Master Series at the end of each season. The WPT international ranking remains the official indicator for the best female and male padel players in the world.

The year 2016 marked 25 years of the International Padel Federation.

AS A DISCIPLINE OF TENNIS, it is only natural that the format of a padel match resembles that of a tennis match. And since the structure of the latter sometimes baffles those who are new to it, so can that of padel. Its rules of play and scoring aren't that straightforward. Unlike football, padel is not about scoring a goal/point and calling 1-0, just as the game is not composed of two evenly timed parts. Therefore, attaining a crystal-clear notion of all aspects of a match is the very first thing to do when getting started with padel. A good way to understand how the game works is to gradually zoom in on the elements of a match. First, look at the overall objective. Second, understand the anatomy of a match, what parts constitute the whole. Third, have in mind the basics you need in order to play. Fourth, memorise the rules so you know what counts and what doesn't. And finally, grasp the ins-and-outs of how to keep the score and define who's the winner.

OBJECTIVE

In a nutshell, the objective of padel is to keep the ball in play for as long as possible, flawlessly hitting it over the net until the opposite team commits a fault. Every time a fault is committed, the other team wins a point. Winning points make the pair win games, and accumulating games helps to win sets. The first team to take two out of the three sets wins the match. Since matches take place in a court much smaller than that of tennis, with walls surrounding the entire perimeter – off which the ball can be played (like in squash) – a less prominent objective of padel is establish a strong and almost intuitive bond with one's partner in order to develop a fluid team dynamic, without which no padel game is won.

MATCH STRUCTURE

Many people grab a padel racquet and step into a court for the physical exercise, the technique practice, or the sheer fun of it – not to compete. But the majority of players, especially amateurs, still get off on the adrenaline rush and excitement of competition provided by a proper match. When that is the case, it becomes imperative to follow a system of scoring and rules.

There are three basic scoring units in every padel match:

• Points: Points begin with one player putting the ball into play by serving, and one of the adversaries receiving. If the ball doesn't clear the net in either of the two serving attempts, the opposing team wins the point. If the ball lands in the service area and the receiver fails to hit it before it bounces twice, the serving team wins the point. If the ball clears the net, lands in the service area, and the opponent returns the serve successfully, the team who manages to keep the ball in play the longest without a) letting it bounce twice, b) hitting it outside the court grounds, c) failing to clear the net, or d) committing other faults wins a point.

• Games: The first team to win four points, with at least a two-point margin, wins the game. The only exception is when both teams draw at three points each. When this happens, the game goes to deuce; the score is set to 40-40 (3-3) and the play continues until one of the teams wins two points in a row – the first point is the advantage, the second is the game. If one of the teams wins a point, they get the advantage. But if the opponents win the following point, the score is reset to 40-40.

• Sets: A set is won when one of the teams scores at least 6 games – provided they lead by at least two games. When teams draw at 5 games each, the set goes to 7 games. If they draw at 6 games each, a tie-break is usually introduced.

While tennis matches are sometimes played as a best out of five sets, padel matches are best out of three.

Though this is the official anatomy of a padel match, oftentimes players use the scoring system but opt to play only a single set. Alternatively, a friendly match could also be played by counting points from 1 to 50, for example. This tends to be an option when the match is time constricted or when the reason for playing is to practice a technique/strategy as opposed to defining a winner.

THE PADEL COURT

Besides 2-4 players, a stringless racquet (or bat), adequate shoes, and properly pressurised balls, the only other essential in a game of padel is a court. Although some padel games are played in singles format, roughly 90% of all courts in the world are designed for doubles format. That is mainly because being such a fast-paced game played in relatively small grounds renders one-on-one matches too difficult. Furthermore, in official, professional-level competitions, such as the World Padel Tour, padel is only played in doubles.

Padel courts are rectangular, and in both singles and doubles the size of the playing area is roughly one-quarter of a tennis court. The official internal measurements of singles courts are 20m x 6m, whereas doubles courts, designed for 4 players, run 20 metres in length and 10 metres in width. At the centre of the rectangle, a 10-metre-long net is suspended at 0.88 metres from the ground, dividing the pitch into two. Capped with a white strip and tensioned by a post in each extremity, this synthetic fibre mesh covers the entire limits of the court.

Either side of the court features a service line, marked parallel to the net and 6.95m away from it. On both sides, a perpendicular line runs in the section between the service line and the net, delimiting the central service line and making both longitudinal halves of the court symmetrical. Lines are usually of white or black colour, depending on the colour of the ground surface, which tends to be blue, terra-cotta, or green. Surfaces can be made of cement, artificial grass, or synthetic material, appropriate for the ball to bounce in a regular manner.

The main distinction between a tennis and padel court is that the latter must be fully enclosed, surrounded by walls of at least 4 metres at the ends and 3 metres on the sides. Back walls can be either opaque or transparent and are usually made of glass, acrylic, or brick. Along the sides, walls often consist of very tense, metallic fences with mesh holes smaller than the balls – but glass is also common. The important element of the walls is that they feature a hard, uniform surface so as to allow the ball to bounce or slide freely, as well as permit bodily contact.

Since high shots are common in padel, the entire extension of the court must be unobstructed and at least 6 metres in height. Likewise, both lateral sides of the court must feature at least one access point near the centre to allow out-of-court play. These borderline sections usually extend for 2 metres in width and 4 metres in length, and are usually kept free of obstacles so players can run out, hit the ball, and run back in safely. Such areas of the perimeter tend to be protected by some kind of anti-shock cushioning to avoid injuries lest any bodily contact occurs. Artificial lighting used in night matches must fall uniformly on the court without affecting the vision of players.

RULES OF PLAY

Whether playing professionally or a in a friendly weekend match with the family, a basic set of rules applies to every match of padel. These are the fundamental principles of the game as per the official International Padel Federation rulebook, and whilst some of them can be overlooked in unofficial practices, being aware of them helps one to navigate all playing formats.

At the start of the match, players should stand with their respective team member on the chosen side of the court. To choose who takes which end, as well as to decide which team serves first, someone should toss a coin. (In professional padel matches, this is usually carried out by an umpire). Whoever wins can either pick their side of the court or serve/receive the first game. If the team opts for a choice of sides, the other pair can decide whether they receive or serve. If the pair prefers to serve/receive, their opponents may select which side to start on. Alternatively, the winner of heads-or-tails can pass on the decision to their opponents. Once the choice has been made, the teams take their positions according to who is serving and receiving.

Regardless of the initial decision, teams must switch sides after every odd game is finished (e.g. 1-0, 4-3, etc.) This is mainly done so both pairs have to deal with the same weather conditions, such as wind or sunlight direction. Before taking their position on the other end, teams are entitled to a brief rest – apart from the very first court swap of each set. These terms are of course flexible in friendly matches, but in professional tournaments, for instance, rest periods are timed to 120 seconds. Once a set is over, a slightly more prolonged rest period is allowed. If the set has ended at an even total of games (e.g. 6-0), teams needn't switch sides when the new set begins. Otherwise, a change of ends should ensue with the start of each new set. During the tie-break, a change of sides occurs at the end of every sixth point.

THE SERVICE/SERVE

Every point starts with a serve, and every server is entitled to two service attempts per point. The server is the player designated to put the ball in play. The player does so by standing with both feet behind the service line on their half of the court (aka service box) until the ball is no longer in contact with the server's racquet. Meanwhile, their partner can stand anywhere on the other half of their side of the court. Stepping on or over the service line, or across the other half of the court before the service is complete, is considered a fault, as are any large/abrupt movements (e.g. jumping or walking) that may affect the accepted position.

To carry out a valid serve, the player should bounce the ball within their service box grounds, making sure to hit it before it bounces over waist-high, whilst keeping at least one foot on the ground. The ball should always fly diagonally, clear the net, and land within the delineated receiving box of the receiver. The first service of each game is taken from the right half of the server's court to the right half of the receiver's court – which, from the server's perspective, represents the left side. After every point, the server switches sides, alternating until the game is over.

Similarly, at the start of the first and second game of each set, the serving team decides which of its team members will be the first to serve – an order which must be followed throughout the set. Should the order be missed, the designated server must take their position straight away and there are no implications to the score. That said, teams cannot deliberately skip the service order – every player must serve in the established order.

Servers should observe their opponents and make sure the receiver is ready before carrying out the service. That said, in any padel match, it is good practice for the receiver to avoid delays and adapt to the server's rhythm. If the server happens to put the ball in play before the receiver is ready, the latter can call "not ready" and have the first serice repeated.

Any infringement upon the aforementioned guidelines will be considered a service fault. Other types of fault are committed if the server accidentally misses the ball or hits it with any part of their body or garments. When the ball lands outside the limits of the receiver's box without even touching the lines, the service is faulty. The same goes for when the ball lands in the valid area and touches the surrounding walls before bouncing a second time, or when it bounces out of court to an area beyond the official safety zone. If a player faults the first service, they may take another. Faulting the second service results in the loss of the point.

An exceptional occurrence during a serve is what the regulation calls "Net Service" or "Let Service." These happen when the ball touches either the cap of the net or the net posts, bounces on the valid receiving area, and is hit by the receiver or touches the ground twice. Calling a "net" or "let" means the service should be repeated, whether it was the first or second attempt. It is important to note that if a let is called on the second service, the player is entitled to only one more attempt. Let can also be called during the point in the event the ball splits open, any object/body (such as a bird or another ball) invades the playing area, or one of the players deliberately or involuntarily disturbs the course of the point. In these cases, also known as interferences, the dispute must stop immediately and the point resumes. In official matches, interferences or calling an inappropriate or invalid "let" can result in the team losing the point.

SERVICE RETURNS

The player receiving the serve is called the receiver. They may stand anywhere on their half of the court within the area designated as the receiving box. Their partner can also choose where to stand, provided they don't breach the delimitations or moves outside the playing area before the serve is carried out. The receiver's objective is to hit the ball that has landed on their receiving box over the net before it bounces twice, directing it anywhere on the adversary's court. They must always allow the ball to bounce once before responding, and therefore cannot volley the serve. If the ball accidentally hits the player, racquet, or garments before touching the ground, it is considered a fault and the point goes to the server.

As with serving, receiving teams have to decide which of the members will be the first to receive. The choice is made in the first game of each set and must be followed until another set begins. This means that if a player of the receiving team opts to stand on the right half of their side of the court, they must always be there when the service is taking place. Also akin to serving rules, all players must receive.

A valid return entails sending the ball over the net to the other side of the court prior to its second bounce. If one of the opponents volleys the return, the ball is in play; same if the ball lands in the opposing court and then bounces off the walls/fences or goes out of court. Returns are also valid if they touch any part of the net or posts before bouncing on the adversary's court. In unusual situations, a player can hit the served ball off the wall of their own side of the court – if it bounces directly into the opponent's court, it is a valid return. Provided that the racquet does not hit the ball twice and detaches from its surface naturally, players are allowed to "push" the ball upon returning a serve.

PLAYING THE POINT (BALL IN PLAY)

A point officially begins after both the serve and the return have taken place according to the rules. From then on, players will hit the ball alternately, always observing the maximum number of bounces per courtside (one) and hits per team (one). When the ball hits any internal section of the walls/fences after its first bounce on the ground, players may hit it over the net to the opponent's side of the court, ensuring it doesn't touch their own playing area a second time. In this context, players are not obliged to take turns hitting the ball in play. As long as they remain within their side of the court and/or out-of-court area, they can play the entire point alone.

The dispute ends when a fault has been committed and the opposing team is awarded the point.

During the point (aka "rally"), players must not allow their bodies, racquets, and/or garments to touch any part of the net or the opponent's court – apart from the door frame when undergoing out-of-court play. If that happens, a fault is committed and the point is given to the adversaries. The same applies when a player hits the ball more than once or the ball touches the ground twice before being returned. Faulty moves also include hitting the ball prior to it crossing the net, throwing the racquet to complete a return, and taking a shot simultaneously with a team member. Both direct and off-the-wall shots will be considered a fault if they hit the fence/wall on the opponent's court before touching the ground at least once. Any bodily contact with the ball will also be considered a fault.

OUT-OF-COURT PLAYS

One of the idiosyncrasies of padel, and perhaps also one of the most exciting moments of a match, is when players step outside of the court boundaries to take a shot. These instances are called "out-of-court play," and they are allowed so long as the player sticks to the delimitations of this specific area and its regulations. More often than not, out-of-court situations happen after one of the players attempts a "lob" (hitting the ball over the opponent standing close to the net) and one of the opponents responds with a "smash". This forceful hit will cause the ball to bounce higher, sometimes enough to go over the sidewalls, urging one of the defensive players to leave the court grounds and attempt to return it before it bounces a second time. It is important to note that for out-of-court play to be authorised, the ball doesn't have to cross to the other side of the fence directly after bouncing on the ground. It can hit the ground on the opposing court, bounce off the wall, and then leave the court. Another important point is that the player taking an out-of-court shot needn't hit the ball over the net – they can direct the shot to go through the door, straight onto the opponent's court.

CHANGE OF BALLS

Whilst this is not a highly influential rule in friendly padel matches, competitions (both at amateur and professional levels) tend to take the act of changing balls rather seriously. That is because, like the racquet, the condition of the balls may affect, even if only slightly, the way some players decide to take shots. Therefore, it is common for the ball change policy, as well as the number of balls per match and their models, to be announced by event organisers. In instances when ball changes take place, they usually occur after a particular number of games or at the start of each set. It is mandatory in competitions, and advised in any type of amateur match, to have at least two balls at hand when beginning a point.

SCORING

One doesn't need to keep score in order to enjoy a game of padel. And even if players decide to keep score, simply counting points as zero, one, two, three, etc. could work as a way to establish competition and define a winner at the end of the match. But those who wish to employ the official padel scoring system or are partaking in a competition will meet a methodology reminiscent of tennis, and thus will need to be familiar with its particular terminology.

In professional competitions, the umpire will announce the game score after every point and the set score at the beginning of each game. Since amateur competitions and friendly matches don't usually have umpires, it's customary for the server to call out the score of the game when they are setting up for the next serve – as opposed to right after the point has ended. Likewise, they can announce the score of the set before serving the first point of each game. This helps players keep track of who is winning, avoiding potential confusion over miscounts. It is important to note that the server's score always comes before the receiver's. Also, when the game score is a draw, players tend to substitute the second number with the word "all." For instance, if each team won one point, the score can be announced as 15-All.

GAMES

In a game, the score is kept in 15s and is counted as such:

• Love: Love is equivalent to zero. Players call "love" when no points have been earned by a particular team in a game.

• 15: Once a team wins a point, their score is 15. If the serving team wins the first point, the game will be at 15-Love, which translates to 1-0. Conversely, if the serving team loses the first point, the score is Love-15.

• 30: The second point won means a score of 30. If the receiving team has won the first two points, the game score will be Love-30 (0-2). If both teams have won two points apiece, the server should call "30 All."

• 40: The 40 represents the third point won. Hence, if the serving team has won three points and the receiving team has won one point, the score will be 40-15, called out as "Forty Fifteen" and not "Forty to Fifteen."

• Game: Provided that there is a margin of two points when one of the teams scores the fourth point, that team wins the game. If the receiving team has won four points in a row and the serving team none, the score will be Love-Game – though players don't usually call that out. The term "game point" refers to that specific point potentially being the last one of the game. The same goes for "set point" and "match point" – the point about to be played can define the set or match.

DEUCE

A deuce is called when the score reaches 40-40, meaning neither team has won four points with a two-point margin. Henceforth, the score switches from 15s to deuce-advantage-game, and teams need to win two points in a row from when deuce is called. For example, if team A wins the point after deuce, they win advantage. And if they win the point after advantage, they will have the margin of two and therefore win the game. But if team A wins the first point and team B wins the second, the game goes back to deuce, and they will keep taking turns until the two-point margin is reached. This back-and-forth makes the deuce an exciting part of the game, but it can also make it tiring, since some can carry on for a long time. When announcing the advantage, the server will commonly say "ad-in" or "my ad" if they have won the advantage point, and "ad-out" or "your ad" if the receiving team is closer to winning the game. In professional matches, umpires tend to call out "Advantage" plus the surname of the respective pair.

SETS

Winning 6 games makes a team win a set – and after sets, the match. As games can only be won when a margin of two points is reached, a team can only win a set if there is a margin of two games between them and their opponent. Therefore, even though sets are marked from 0 to 6, if both teams win 5 games each, the margin will not be reached unless another game is added to the set. Ergo, a set can have a score of 6-0 as well as 9-7, since in both cases the winning team has won by a margin equal or higher than two games. Practically speaking, this means that in order to get the two-game margin, a team needs to "break" at least one of their opponent's service games in the set.

TIE-BREAK

A tie-break means just what it is: the goal is to break the tie, or more specifically, the tie in a set. This occurs when neither team has managed to maintain the two-game margin and the score draws at 6-6. Tiebreakers are an alternative to counting up games until the margin is established and a way to curb the set from extending too much; a kind of sudden death. It is to the discretion of players (or the regulations of the event) to determine whether to adopt a tiebreaker once the score comes to six-all. That said, tie-breaks tend to be chosen over regular deuce sets.

Unlike games, tiebreakers are counted per points, not 15s. Teams need to get seven points to win the tiebreaker, but they still need to meet a two-point margin. Hence, a tie-break score can be 7-1 or 7-5. But it can also come up to 22-21. Points are called out per usual, with the server announcing the score as they are readying to serve. The server will call "Five-Two" if they are winning 5-2 and "Two-Five" if they are losing.

Different from the deuce, tie-breaks incur a constant switch of the server. The first player/team to serve in a tie-break is the one due to have served the thirteenth game. Once the first point ends, regardless of who wins it, a change of service takes place. From then on, the server switches every two points. Before the seventh point is played, the teams switch sides, doing so again before the fourteenth point and twenty-first point are played until the tie-break ends. Once a new set begins, the team who held the service on the game prior to the tiebreaker serves the first game.

ALTERNATIVE SCORING

Besides the official method of scoring, there are other alternative ways to structure a match so it remains competitive, follows customary practices, and suits your needs. Alternative scoring methods, such as the Super Tie-break, help with shortening the duration of a match whilst maintaining an officiality to it. This mode functions as a substitute for the third and last set when the match is at a 1-1 draw. The main difference between a regular tiebreaker and a super tie-break is that the latter is won by reaching 10 points as opposed to 7 – as long as the two-point margin is reached. Hence, the winners of the super tie-break are the winning team of the match. Similarly, some people opt to play what is called a "mini-set" instead of a set or a full match. A mini-set follows the same style of scoring as a normal set, though it is only played until one of the teams wins four games, respecting the two-game margin. If there is a draw at 4-4, a standard tie-break decides the match.

READING SCORES

A scoreboard is the visual representation of the status of a padel match. It breaks down the punctuation by columns, with each strip showing the number of games won in a particular set and each line representing a team. Scoreboards are usually featured in professional competitions, administered by the umpire, and displayed at the top left corner of the TV screen as such:

Team A 6 5 7 (11)
Team B 3 7 6

The above example indicates that the first set was won with a margin of 3 games, while the second set was a deuce set, hence both teams drew at 5-5. The third set went a similar way: team A and B won 6 games each, which led to a tiebreaker. The number 11 in parentheses tells the lower tie-break score – as per usual with line scoring systems – meaning Team A won 13-11, reaching the two-point margin. Tie-break points are thus shown because if the winner had won by 7-2, it would be difficult to guess exactly how many points the losing team won.

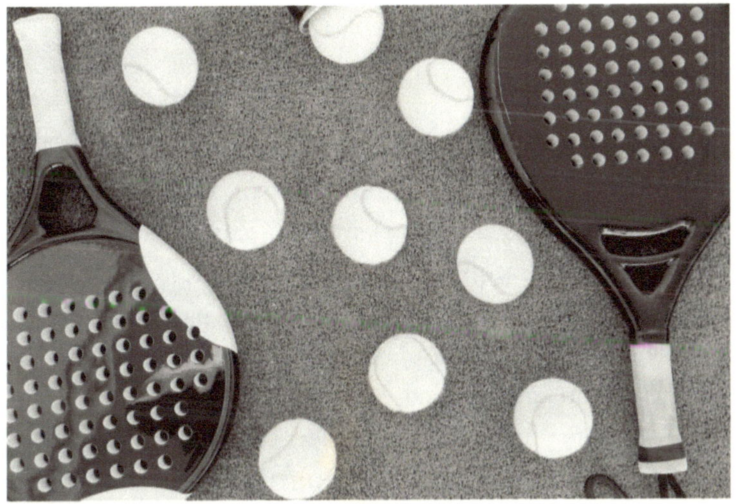

PADEL IS A RELATIVELY simple sport that doesn't require much more than an official court, a racquet (also known as a paddle or bat), and a ball. Some people like to dress up, spend a lot of money on top-range equipment, and wear all sorts of accessories. But these can also prove to be a hindrance, and in a game like padel, where agility and flexibility counts, you want to feel as nimble as possible. The truth is, a racquet that feels good in your hand and matches your technique is better than a well-marketed one. Balls that are properly pressured and not frayed will do the job. Good-quality, comfortable shoes are also important, as they protect your feet and help with shock absorption when you sprint outside the court or jump high to hit that smash. The bottom line is, although there is a wide range of equipment and accessories to choose from, choosing the most suitable to your needs, build, and skill level is what helps you improve your game.

PADEL RACQUETS

Despite technological developments in material and design, Padel racquets have a very long lifespan. One could take a bat they haven't used in years and still play a match without problems. With racquets, their condition and/or quality are secondary to the way they work for each particular player, e.g., whether they get the shots to the direction and with the technique you have applied.

The very first padel racquets were but perforated wooden paddles borrowed from American Platform Tennis. This was mainly because of similarities in court size and ball type between both sports. With time, the padel industry developed designs of its own, increasing the surface of contact and eventually introducing new materials such as plywood and aluminium, coated with variations of rubber paint and fibreglass. Later, advances in technology allowed manufacturers to build stronger and lighter racquets out of carbon and other similar materials. At the same time the concept of "signature models" arose, so did the rubber core paddles, which brought power and speed to a whole new level. Since then, the majority of padel racquets have been made with synthetic materials, and though the majority are still designed and produced in Argentina and Spain, manufacturing has also expanded to Asia.

Luckily for padel players, their racquets don't have strings. This is probably one of the main differences between padel and tennis equipment, and one of the most befuddling aspects of the latter. Therefore, padel racquets consist of two main elements/parts: the head and the handle – both of which have to comply with the official manufacturing regulations. The handle of a paddle cannot be more than 20 centimetres in length, 50 millimetres in width, and 50 millimetres in thickness. The head, on the other hand, may vary in length – provided it does not exceed 45.5 centimetres when combined with the handle. Width-wise, the head can stretch for a maximum of 26 centimetres, whereas its thickness shouldn't measure more than 38 millimetres. These measurements, though merely a formality at first glimpse, can have practical effects worthy of consideration when choosing a racquet for your particular anatomy.

Another component of a padel bat is the impact surface. This is dotted by several tiny holes (averaging 10 millimetres in diameter, depending on their position in relation to the edge of the racquet) whose primary purpose is to lessen the air resistance and render the racquet more aerodynamic. The surfaces on either side are always flat, but they may have a rough or smooth texture depending on the model. Besides accessories to assist in weight distribution, post-hit vibration, and the mandatory non-elastic wrist band that is attached to the handle, racquets cannot have any other devices attached to them. Nor can they feature any sort of reflective material or noisy add-ons which may disturb other players. Whilst this may sound like a very restrictive and uniform regulation, there are still a plethora of different designs out there.

CHOOSING A PADEL RACQUET

Though buying a padel racquet isn't a mammoth task, it does require attention to detail, knowledge of one's style and skill level, and a bit of technical savvy – to say nothing of one's budget, of course. Sure, anyone can have fun playing a weekend match with any old bat. But when taking a step further into the world of padel and buying your own gear, the aforementioned considerations should be heeded. That said, given the current overall quality of materials, one will rarely find something "bad" when purchasing a new racquet. There may be alternatives made from more high-tech and durable materials, but most of them do the most cardinal job of padel: hitting the ball over the net.

Another thing to keep in mind when choosing a racquet is that nothing can be more enlightening than a trial run. Regardless of what the salesperson says, what the top pro players are using, or what you read on a review, trying before buying will allow you to have a real feel of what the equipment is like. Fortunately, many stores have spare racquets which they set aside especially for play-test. So, before investing in new material, it is a good idea to make inquiries and take your time experimenting with as many paddles as you need.

Unlike tennis, where players tend to have more than one racquet lest the strings break, padel enthusiasts can make do with a single bat for most of their journey. Perhaps a second racquet will come in handy when joining competitions and travelling for matches, but at the beginning, more than building a collection, one should strive to find the right type of racquet – and that will mean observing factors such as shape, weight, and material.

PADEL RACQUET TYPES

Among the main factors that distinguish the types of padel racquets is the shape of their heads. Paddles are composed of two symmetrical surfaces (known as plates or faces) that are either round, drop, or diamond-shaped, with each shape bearing pros and cons in terms of performance, depending on the player and skill level. Beyond aesthetics, the shape of the head is directly related to weight distribution and balance, or the racquet's centre of gravity. This is measured and referred to by the position of the heaviest point in relation to the bottom of the handle. Therefore, if a racquet has a low balance, it means its weight distribution falls toward the handle. A racquet featuring a centred balance (or "on par") translates to having the majority of its weight concentrated on the region where the handle meets the head. Alternatively, a racquet with high balance has a heavy head, and its centre of gravity sits toward the top

• Round Shape: With its centre of balance near the

handle, this version is a favourite among beginners. It is nick-named the "control racquet" because its weight distribution makes it easy to wield and stabilise a firm grip, thus facilitating control when taking a shot. Conversely, the relatively light head decreases the drive when striking the ball, rendering shots generally less powerful and fast. This becomes particularly evident when attempting smashes. Round-shaped racquets feature a broader sweet spot than their counterparts, which means players can get away with not hitting the ball in the centre of the impact surface. This makes the model popular among highly skilled and professional defensive players whose priority is ball placement over power.

• Drop Shape: Also known as the Teardrop Shape, this kind of racquet has a centred balance and stands on the middle ground between control and power. The even weight distribution makes it feel balanced and easy to swing. This means that technique-wise, players are able to employ all sorts of effects in various scenarios and game speeds. Hence, they are the most popular type of paddle – an intermediate player's go-to choice.

• Diamond Shape: With most of its weight being distributed toward the top of the paddle, diamond-shaped models have a high centre of balance. This allows the racquet to gain momentum when driving for the ball, which favours power shots. On the other hand, diamond paddles have a minimal sweet spot – one has to hit the ball with the very centre of the impact surface. They are also trickier to manipulate, so the ability to control movement can be compromised more easily. That is why the majority of players using these bats have higher levels of experience and a refined technique. Professionals with attack-oriented styles of play are particularly fond of this shape. Those who are in the process of switching to a diamond racquet should consider starting out with a lighter model in order to get used to the weight shift.

WEIGHT

Weight is yet another important element in any paddle. Thanks to high-tech materials, nowadays most racquets can be considered light and manufacturers rarely produce something that is overly difficult to handle. Nevertheless, a few grams here or there can make it feel completely different to grip – especially during a long rally.

Common sense would compel heavier, stronger players to pick heavier racquets and lighter players with less physical strength to opt for light gear. Still, as a rule of thumb, one should seek a paddle with the right amount of heft to not feel heavy; something light enough that you can swing with ease and comfort but heavy enough to drive the ball with speed. In general, male players use paddles in the 360g to 390g range, with 370g being the most common. Female players tend to use racquets that weigh anywhere between 340g and 370g. Meanwhile, children up to the age of fifteen wouldn't play with anything heavier than 280g.

It's important to note that weight and balance are distinct aspects. A bat weighing 350g with a low balance will feel and respond differently than one with the same weight but a high balance. Likewise, a 350g racquet with a low balance will provide more control than a 330-gram one with a high balance. This makes weight a highly subjective matter, more dependent on your own physical structure and strength. That's another reason to try it before choosing.

Experience level also matters when figuring out how heavy a racquet you need. Beginners, for instance, are encouraged to seek lighter paddles, developing technique and learning how to control those first – even if they could potentially use something heavier. Once a degree of comfort has been reached, you'll naturally feel like it's time to step up. Making this a gradual change can be significant in staying motivated throughout the first learning steps, as opposed to struggling with the equipment and not moving forward.

Weight also plays a role in causing and avoiding injuries. Using too light of a racquet generally means it will vibrate more upon impact and that your arm will aid more in supporting the load. In the long run, the constant shock absorption can harm joints and tendons. Moreover, lighter racquets tend to be less durable and thus easier to break. Heavier paddles, on the other hand, may injure the elbows, wrists, and shoulders of players whose muscles aren't conditioned for their weight. Besides, a racquet that is too heavy will automatically decrease the player's reflexes, which can prove an issue, especially with volleys.

GRIP

The grip is the cylindrical area below the shaft, the section where you grab the racquet. Though this aspect is often underestimated, any experienced player will vouch for the importance of grips. Nonetheless, there isn't an objective criterion for finding the right grip size. Again, it is a matter of comfort. Even someone with big hands and long fingers may prefer a slender grip. The best alternative, then, is to try both extremes – one with a large diameter and another with a short diameter. If still uncertain, a general tip from tennis players is to go for a thickness that allows you to touch the top bit of your middle finger with the tip of your thumb when grabbing the racquet. Whatever the case, extra thin grips should be avoided. Beginners are particularly inclined to choose such dimensions because it feels easier to manipulate the racquet, but they also can make one more susceptible to racquet slips and twists, and those can cause wrist injuries. That said, if the decision between two diameters seems too difficult, going with the slenderer one turns out to be the right solution since it is possible to increase its thickness by adding grip tape. Indeed, grip tape (or overgrip) should be changed regularly to maintain adhesion and keep away foul smells. However, it is important to keep in mind that increasing the thickness of the handle alters its weight, consequently influencing the entire balance of the racquet.

MATERIALS

The material of a padel racquet has an effect on the durability of the equipment as well as its hardness, or "flexibility". In this case, flexibility refers to how bouncy the material is. This index is often found on the packaging under the term "ball output". Racquets with high ball outputs tend to have impact surfaces off which the ball can spring more actively. Such materials are recommended to beginners and players with less strength, since it requires less effort to hit the ball over to the other side.

When it comes to materials, paddles have two different sections: the frame and the core. The two main materials used in frames are fibreglass and carbon. Being cheaper to produce, fibreglass is common in lower-end models, whereas carbon is the material of choice (sometimes combined with Kevlar) for high-end and more costly equipment. Also, being less rigid, fibreglass racquets usually present good flexibility, providing more acceleration than carbon bats and cushioning the impact more effectively. Carbon, on the other hand, weighs less and renders a more solid structure than fibreglass paddles, consequently making the equipment last longer.

As for core materials, the type of composition generally varies between foam (polyurethane) and EVA rubber. Texture-wise, the first features a rougher surface with tiny bubbles whilst the latter is completely smooth. To grasp their role and importance, it is good to think of the core of a paddle as the strings of a tennis racquet – it is what propels the ball and controls its release and effects. Foam, due to its soft, airy compound, renders the paddle more flexible. This allows the player to really feel the ball springing off the racquet. Because of the increased flexibility, a smaller amount of power will still prove enough to keep the ball in play. Also related to its flexible properties, a polyurethane surface will have a relatively long contact with the ball before releasing it, which facilitates control and the use of effects. Meanwhile, EVA possesses resistance as its main feature. Here, that means not only more durability but also resistance to impact, which translates to its anti-vibration quality. This kind of compound can be subdivided into hard and soft. Hard EVA racquets are at their optimum in high-speed and powerful movements and are thus more suitable for experienced players. Since the contact period with the ball is short, the racquet drives the shot with intensity, producing more speed. Conversely, soft EVA resembles foam compounds in that it generates more control and feeling to the strike. However, having less flexibility compared to polyurethane, as well as a smoother texture, compromises control and the ability to create effects when hitting the ball with lots of power.

PRICE RANGE

Though the majority of people, especially those starting out, have a budget in mind when purchasing a padel racquet, it shouldn't be the main factor in the decision – leastwise because it will probably be a long-term investment. In other words, it's much better to spend a bit more at first to have a piece of equipment that will last several months and suits your level than save on the purchase and return to the store a couple of months later. Therefore, the aforementioned play-test is of the essence. Try several shapes, brands, weights, and materials, both within and slightly over your budget so as to compare higher-end with lower-end models.

Generally, prices begin at €50 for the most elementary paddle, with top-quality ones costing as much as €300.
- Bullpadel Libra 2021 EVA (Round, 350g): €70
- Starvie Metheora Junior Foam: €70
- Babolat Counter Vertuo 2021 EVA (Tear, 350g): ~ €150
- Adidas Essnova Carbon 3.0 2021 (Diamond, 360g): ~ €200

• Volt 900V Carbon (Tear, 370g): ∼ €275

THE PADEL BALL

At first glance, padel balls look like tennis balls. And in fact, aesthetically, they are much alike: both are made of a rubber sphere of approximately 6.5 centimetres in diameter and roughly 57 grams, enclosed by a yellowish felt exterior. The main difference is the internal pressure. According to IPF standards, padel balls should feature between 4.6 kg and 5.2 kg per 2.54 square cm, which makes them about 0.06 less pressurised than tennis balls. This factor slows the ball some-what, playing a huge role in the pace of a padel match, where court dimensions are much smaller than tennis. Official regulations also require the bounce property to be anywhere between 135 and 145 centimetres when dropped from 2.54 metres onto a hard surface. If a match is happening 500 metres above sea level, a slightly different type of ball, with lower bounce, can be used.

Black Crown, Head, Adidas, and Dunlop are some of the major ball manufacturers. Whilst the majority of players wouldn't be able to notice the difference between brands, hitting a brand new ball and a frayed, old one are two very different feelings. Likewise, paying attention to the type of court the ball has been designed for can prove more useful than choosing a ball according to the brand.

Padel balls come in boats (or tubes) of three and range between €3 and €8 in price. However, it is not uncommon to see package deals of three boats for €12 or special bulk-buy offers of 72 balls for €100. Beginners or weekend players will find that balls last a couple of months under moderate play.

Those playing two or more times per week will notice the ball's condition deteriorating after 2-3 weeks. All players should consider always having at least three balls handy for a match, and one brand-new boat in case of loss or damage. Also, players should make sure there are no balls on the ground before the beginning of each point, as these present a hazard and can disturb the course of the dispute.

PADEL SHOES

It may not be evident, but padel is a "leg sport" as much as an "arm sport." Though sideways displacement and sliding are not as common as in clay tennis, padel players are constantly moving, sprinting forward and diagonally, halting abruptly, changing direction, and hopping and jumping. Therefore, it would be fair to say that shoes are almost as important as racquets. And that said, playing a match of padel on any given trainers is not recommended.

Indeed, footwear has a huge and direct influence on performance – as well as in avoiding feet and ankle injuries. The right kind of shoes gives you more freedom to move. However, the protection aspect should inform the greatest part of your decision when purchasing new padel footwear. Other points to consider are comfort, flexibility, material durability, and, to a lesser extent, aesthetics.

At first glance, padel shoes look similar to tennis shoes; their general shape resembles each other a lot. But that doesn't mean they could be used interchangeably. Manufacturers have developed shoes especially for the practice of padel, with a specific kind of sole that provides enough grip for the constant stops-and-starts. Because surface types vary from court to court, the majority of padel shoes nowadays are designed to consider the traction factor. Most models also have reinforced heel notches and top lines in order to stabilise the ankle and minimise the potential of sprains. A lot of attention is also given to the knees, one of the body parts that suffers the most impact. To address that, padel shoes generally adopt a layered cushioning system comprised of a combination of gel sole, midsole, and innersole. Such a soft underside consequently provides a light step and a springy sensation in explosive starts.

There are three main types of soles: omni, plug, and mixed.

• Omni soles are designed to grip the surface and therefore aren't suitable for clay courts or playing fields that invite sliding. Models with omni-tread patterns are good for quick and sudden movements, such as dashes to and from the net.

• Plug soles are highly functional for sliding and stretching. They are often abrasion-resistant and tend to last longer than their omni counterparts, adhering well to synthetic surfaces.

• Mixed soles bring the best of both worlds. They are usually split in half lengthwise, with the internal front section of the sole featuring an omni pattern, which enhances adherence, while the back of the sole is dotted with plugs to facilitate sliding.

CHOOSING PADEL SHOES

Padel shoes tend to have a lifespan of 130-160 hours and it is easy to determine their condition just by glancing at the soles. If the patterns of the undersides have lost their cavities, it means that a replacement is imminent. Many players, especially those who compete, have two pairs of shoes of the same model – one for light training and friendly matches and the other for competitions. It is advisable, however, to break in brand-new shoes in brief games instead of the full three sets so as to prevent blisters and familiarise yourself with the step.

Shoes for padel are a median investment. Brands abound, with the popular Adidas, Asics, Kswiss, and Lotto being the standard. Low-end and junior shoes can be purchased for as little as €30. Adult models start at €50 and may cost up to €200. It is possible to find good-quality footwear for around €100. When looking to buy a new pair, besides paying attention to the outsole, the general rule is that the size should be exactly right and the shoe should feel both comfortable and secure.

Other factors to keep in mind:

• Cushioning: With so much starting and stopping on hard surfaces, impact shocks are ubiquitous in padel. Hence, the ideal pair of shoes should have the sort of cushioning that renders the act of stepping a soft and gradual move, as opposed to a thud.

• Heel cups: When trying on a pair of shoes, it is important that the heel remains locked in place and doesn't slide up or down with every step. Different heights and concavity depths influence just how firmly the heel sits and thus how stable the ankle remains.

• Toe caps: Toe caps in padel shoes are not as pronounced as in tennis shoes – but they are still a mandatory feature throughout all models. This extra layer of rubber sheltering the toes works more as a protection for the shoes themselves, since players tend to drag their feet between steps or strokes.

• Removable insoles: Just like everyday sneakers may need an extra insole to feel more comfortable, the use of an extra layer of cushioning – or a more orthotic version – can add the extra bit of comfort needed to avoid long-term foot problems.

PADEL CLOTHING

Besides the racquet and shoes, all other padel equipment can be considered secondary when it comes to performance. Any other gear a player chooses to use or wear becomes more a matter of comfort – and that applies to padel clothing. Whilst any old cotton T-shirt and loose-fitting shorts are suitable for a weekend match, people who are in the padel court a few times per week and/or compete regularly tend to opt for niche products. In this sense, the basic padel costume is very similar to that of tennis and other racquet sports: a T-shirt, shorts, and socks.

Design-wise, short-sleeve T-shirts allow your arms and elbows to move and flex freely. (Note that wearing sleeveless garments in official competitions is against the IPF regulation). For this same reason, it is a good idea to refrain from wearing tight tops, as they may restrict shoulders and back. Likewise, shorts should leave room for your legs to spread in all directions, and having the leg opening cut above the knee helps with that. Selecting a model with an elasticized waistband and a drawstring (as opposed to buttons or zippers) also enhances comfort. Another factor that is taken for granted when choosing the ideal padel shorts is the pockets. These are essential for storing balls when training, as well as competing. Fortunately, the vast majority of padel-oriented models will come with at least two pockets. Socks vary between invisible, low-cut, anklets, and crew, and it is up to each player to decide which works best depending on footwear.

When it comes to material, it is important to observe both the comfort it provides and how suitable it is for the given weather conditions. Many padel T-shirts are made of breathable, fast-drying materials, usually a mix of polyester and elastane. The same goes for shorts and sometimes socks. These compositions tend to be lightweight and are ideal for warmer climates, where wearing a cotton T-shirt would block transpiration. The opposite is true for colder climates. Manufacturers have developed a range of garments that store body heat, which is particularly useful when having several rest breaks between games and/or during training. Most thermal clothing comes as close-fitting, long-sleeve T-shirts and leggings. Although these may compromise comfort and flexibility, keeping the body warm throughout the practice helps prevent injuries. Padel players mainly wear fleeces, jumpers, and jackets during warm-up/cool-down in colder days, but seldom in the match itself. That said, it is always a good idea to carry a warmer piece of clothing to put on afterwards, especially if playing at night.

Last but not least, the colour of garments is another (oft-underestimated) aspect to consider when choosing padel clothing. Whilst in official tournaments it is mandatory for pairs to wear uniforms of the same colour, informal padel practice has no such rules. To many, it comes down to aesthetics and personal preferences. But especially when playing on warm days under the sun, the colour of T-shirts can have a direct impact on performance. That is why, in general, players opt for light-coloured or white garments. Such a dress code may have a symbolic value reminiscent of tennis, but in most cases, it is a practical matter of choosing clothes that reflect light and heat.

Prices vary according to brand, material technology, and special features such as collars and double lining. But it is possible to get a basic set (T-shirt plus shorts) for around €40 on special. T-shirts range between €20 to €50, whereas shorts usually cost around €30. Basic socks often come in pairs of three at roughly €10 for a set. More high-tech options can be purchased individually for around €8.

PADEL ACCESSORIES

One can get carried away with the amazing amount and variety of accessories found in padel stores. But anyone who has been playing for a while can confirm that, ultimately and essentially, most accessories are what they are – extras. And in many cases, these don't have to be niche padel products to have the desired effect. E.g., a regular sports hat will do the same job as a "padel hat." Nonetheless, amidst unnecessary gadgets, some accessories play a more fundamental role when preparing for a match.

• Hats and Visors: This is probably the most common and useful accessory for padel players. The sun is often a factor to take into account, and hats/visors help to protect the skin whilst blocking the rays from hitting the eyes, which could have repercussions on performance. Caps are the most popular type of hats, mainly due to being so practical, inexpensive, and adjustable. The colour guideline also applies for caps, with light tones recommended for daytime play. That said, dark-coloured brims help minimise glare. Beyond sun protection, hats also come in handy for keeping perspiration and hair off the face and eyes. On scorching hot days, many players periodically wet their hats as a means to cool down. Prices usually start at €12.

• Sunscreen: Also related to sun protection, sunscreen is a valuable accessory for daytime practices in any kind of weather. After all, UV rays damage the skin even when it is overcast. That is particularly the case for those who play frequently and tend to spend hours on the court. As a rule of thumb, the lighter the skin and the brighter the day, the higher the SPF. Prices vary according to the protection factor.

• Sunglasses: Though not as common as hats, sunglasses are also an effective way of ensuring your vision is not impaired by the sun's rays. Nowadays, there is a wide range of sports sunglasses to choose from, lightweight frames specially designed to sit still on the head during active practices. Still, however useful sunglasses are in minimising glare, many models, especially cheaper ones, tend to fog up. So, if choosing to wear them, it is important to select something that will help, not hinder. Good quality pairs start at €100.

• Headbands and Wristbands: Perspiration is indeed a major issue in all racquet sports since sweaty palms make gripping the racquet more difficult, and a sweaty forehead impairs the vision. The main purpose of headbands and wristbands is to avoid such distraction by soaking sweat; and, in the case of headbands, making sure no strands of hair fall in the player's eyes. These accessories last a long time, are easy to care for, and are relatively cheap: between €4 and €15.

• Towels: Towels are perhaps the simplest, cheapest, and

most effective way of dealing with the aforementioned perspiration issue. Having a 100% cotton towel to dry hands, face, and racquet handle during rest breaks ensures a firm grip at the start of each game and no sweat dripping into the eyes.

MOST PEOPLE FIND out about padel through acquaintances or by coming across an open tournament at the local club. But however the first contact unfolds, few people get started with padel lessons. Instead, they will borrow, buy, or rent a padel racquet and balls, dig out some old shoes, find three other people to join in a game, and book a court. They will then consult a more experienced player to learn more about the rules, but rarely will they make inquiries into the specifics of technique. It seems – and to a certain extent, it is – like a rather intuitive game: you hit the ball over the net.

Indeed, this DIY approach has the benefit of not setting boundaries, of allowing one to fall in love with the sport and learn to walk with their own feet, so to speak. And since padel is much easier to pick up than tennis or squash, the vast majority of beginners will find themselves having lots of fun even if they are not holding the racquet properly or if their court positioning is not tactically advantageous. Whilst with tennis most rookies will enrol in weekly lessons from the outset, it is not uncommon to find padel enthusiasts playing on a weekly basis without any formal training for years on end. That said, there will always come a time when one needs a bit of guidance to reach the next level. After all, one of the greatest thrills of any sport is to witness yourself getting better at it.

Whether taking lessons or not, there are a few important things to keep in mind when setting off on the padel journey. These pieces of the puzzle should be learned sooner rather than later; they are less of rules and more of advice to assist in developing your game without compromising the carefree, fun quality so inherent to padel.

One of the very first elements to take notice of is the "wall game." If a person has never played racquet sports before, or especially if they are coming from tennis, the walls of a padel court may feel confusing. Suddenly there is a new dimension added to the game and players cannot avoid it, try as they may. Squash players may have more facility getting a hang of it, but the dynamics involved and the technique required to master the wall game in padel is still very different. Therefore, it is crucial that beginners learn how the rebound works – and how to work with it – right from the start. Achieving a certain level of comfort when playing off the walls/glass will make a huge positive difference in their learning curve, ultimately assisting in every other aspect of the game. So even if using the wall may seem daunting at first, all players should exercise their confidence and adjust their mindset and game plan from the very beginning to make it feel natural.

A change in perception is also needed for anyone who is about to hit a ball with a racquet for the first time – or for those who have experience playing tennis and squash. Thumping the ball with all one's strength is tempting and often seems like the way to go to win a point. However, it should be stressed that whilst sometimes a player will utilise force in a stroke, padel is not about power. In fact, as experienced players would corroborate, too much power will hinder more than help – especially if the technique is not right. Hence, beginners should try to contain their excitement and aim to develop control instead of power. Taking it step-by-step, learning how to place the ball and use the walls, and fostering a strategic approach to your game will mean that when the time comes to apply force, the shots will be much more effective.

Another essential mindset switch is the notion that one is not alone. Again, unlike tennis and squash, padel is always a team sport played in doubles. Any successful point, game, or match relies on team effort. This utterly fundamental aspect is indeed one of the things that makes padel so fun and popular. And, being fundamental, it means that it should be something that remains ingrained in a player's psyche throughout their practice. After all, establishing a good relationship with your partner goes beyond a tactical requirement. It is often through mutual support and encouragement that players keep in-tune to overcome difficult situations in a match, or to remind themselves to keep having fun.

On a more technical note, beginners should also observe – and nurture – the consistency of their shots. In padel, a good performance often amounts to keeping the ball in play. And keeping the ball in play translates to getting another ball into the opponent's court. Not only will this increase the chances of your adversaries committing a fault, but thinking from a novice standpoint also allows you to repeat your strokes and practice your technique. In the long run, being a consistent player will help you to better position yourself in the court, shift to offensive play with ease, and score the point. It can also assist in tiring your adversaries both physically and mentally. The bottom line is, striving to get one more ball in will improve your skills and move you closer to your tactical objective.

Last but not least, every player should consider investing time and energy in learning the padel technique. This includes everything from how to hold the racquet to striking the ball with the different types of shots and placing yourself on the court. Whether you're taking lessons at the local club, watching matches on TV, getting tips from a friend, or watching video tutorials, having a basic knowledge of the proper technique will improve your overall performance, as well as lessen the chances of developing bad habits. Despite the game requiring little technical level at first, padel players who begin unguided will eventually notice that some things are simply not working. And even if the so-called "right way" does not feel right for you, being aware of it is better than overlooking it completely. After all, technical know-how can be the springboard for having even more fun.

Besides these initial suggestions, there are more technical aspects every player who wants to get better at padel should, at some point, give heed to.

THE GRIP

Before even thinking about taking a shot, a player needs to have the racquet in their hand and (ideally) stand in a ready position. In padel, there are two different denotations to the word grip. The first makes reference to the part of the racquet just above the "butt cap", also called the handle. The other is understood by the fashion in which a player holds the padel racquet when hitting the ball. At first glance, beginners may deem the latter a mere detail. But as a structural facet in technique, it has a significant impact both on how you strike the ball and how your arm (wrist, forearm, elbow) reverberates the blow.

One could argue that the best way to grip the racquet is whatever feels comfortable. And although this is the case to a certain extent (you wouldn't want to adopt anything that doesn't feel right), it may not be effective to make a choice purely based on comfort. Indeed, nothing stops you from switching the grip around, as tennis players often do. But since the game of padel is much faster and the ball travels from racquet to racquet much more quickly, players don't always have the time to fiddle with their grip during rallies.

Therefore, the majority of people tend to choose one grip and stick to it. This is particularly relevant to novices who are in the process of getting used to the pace of the game and perfecting their technique. That said, when you reach a higher technical level, it may make sense to rotate the racquet slightly for a specific shot.

The standard grip in padel is called continental grip. It is also known as the "hammer grip" or the "shaking hands grip" since the action is very similar. Your fingers should wrap around the entirety of the handle, with the index finger (at least) touching the tip of the thumb and the heel of your right/left palm touching the bottom of the handle. As a matter of security, your hand should be through the loop. This is a mandatory practice in official matches but highly recommended on any occasion, lest you end up releasing the racquet during a smash, for instance.

There are several reasons why the continental grip is the most adopted. First, it is convenient and versatile in that it doesn't require any change between forehand and backhand shots or volleys and smashes. Anatomically speaking, it is also the most natural way in which to hold the padel racquet. E.g., your arm and wrist are always in line, hardly in a twisted position. Consequently, a solid continental grip is a good way to prevent notorious elbow injuries. Given the angle of the racquet in relation to the player's hand, a firm continental grip also makes it easier to take low shots that come close to the ground. Since the hitting surface will invariably point upwards, the player will not need to spin the racquet around to direct the stroke above the net. Besides being ideal for flat strokes, the angle of a continental grip also favours effects such as backspin. And since this firm hand position rarely needs adjustments, it gives the player a great advantage when approaching the net to volley – a moment when reflex is of the essence.

Even so, the continental grip may not be ideal for some beginners, particularly children, who sometimes don't have the strength to perform the technique to the T. In these cases, it is possible to start with the most comfortable position and work your way toward the continental grip, making minor adjustments here and there. That way, a solid grip is developed more intuitively and without causing harm to the body. Likewise, professional players often find different types of grips more suitable for specific situations, especially when applying certain effects. Still, they most likely began by mastering the continental grip – it is truly the best starting point to hone your technique.

COURT POSITIONING

The way players move in the court is often just as underestimated as the way they grip the racquet. And yet, as watching a World Padel Tour match will show, moving in and out of specific positions is fundamental – if not crucial – to any padel match. That is because padel is very much dictated by a constant attack-and-defence dynamic with more active rallies, as opposed to the more passive ones often witnessed in tennis. Usually, a team will win the point by forcing their opponents to commit a fault. And the only way to do that, besides waiting for them to fail, is to apply pressure. In padel, pressure (or attack) is a synonym for "net game." And the net game is the most effective way to win points.

Beginners will often wait for the ball to reach them, or

else only move to/from positions according to where the ball has bounced. They tend to pay too much attention to the shot itself and little attention to the position wherein they find themselves. And although the first is essential to making sure the ball reaches the other side, understanding this attack-defence dance can be just as useful when you're starting out as performing the right technique in a groundstroke. This basic knowledge will ensure that when you get to a more advanced level, you will be able to make decisions based upon your opponent's positions, the direction of your shots, and the position of your partner, and react optimally to all scenarios.

Likewise, moving in coordination with your partner has a huge influence on how your game unfolds. Teams should move as one, either mirroring or responding to the other's positioning, depending on where the ball is going to/coming from and whether they are carrying out offensive or defensive play. As a joke that holds truth, coaches often say that padel teams should simulate the movement of a windshield wiper on the court. Indeed, moving independently is one of the biggest mistakes in padel, especially amongst beginners. After all, this allows for the creation of open spaces on your side of the court, and that is precisely where your opponents will direct their shots. Hence, when a player moves near the side wall to hit the ball, their partner should move in the same direction, ensuring the gap between them in the centre of the court is filled. On the other hand, if the ball happens to come toward the middle section, players should try to take turns in hitting it or work out some kind of signal system to avoid bumping into each other. This situation is fairly common in both attack and defence positions, so keeping an eye out for the ball as well as your partner is essential to succeeding as a team.

DEFENSIVE PLAY

In a standard defensive position, like the one taken when returning service, both players are at the back together, one on each side of the court roughly one step behind the service line and two steps away from the side wall, and ready to hit the ball after it has bounced. In these situations, it is not uncommon for defence players to wait for the ball to bounce off the walls before hitting it across the net. Given the distance from the net, it is difficult to win points from the defence zone. Therefore, players will usually opt for control as opposed to power strokes, with the thought of carrying on the point and creating the opportunity to switch to a position of attack. This tends to happen when hitting a good lob and pushing the adversaries to the back of their court. In such occasions, there is enough time to come forward to the net and ready for attack.

OFFENSIVE PLAY

An offensive position, also called a "volley position", is assumed when both players come up to the net. Shots taken from these areas will most likely be volleys, i.e., they won't touch the ground. To set up for offensive play, players should stand roughly in the centre of the serving box. From this position, one can move forward to hit the shot (if it's a short volley) whilst also covering the back of the court. Standing too close to the net gives your opponents room to attempt a lob, which would require you to spring back to collect it and potentially lose the chance to attack. Conversely, standing too far back can put you in a predicament since that is the area where the ball coming from the defence players tends to land. Offensive positions may feel especially intimidating for beginners, for these involve lots of reflexes and potential back-and-forth sprints, but building confidence in the net game and working on volley technique can truly make or break a match.

TECHNICAL FUNDAMENTS

The technique in padel refers specifically to the body-plus-racquet movement a player carries out to hit the ball. Although everyone does this differently, employing their own style and idiosyncrasies, there is a standard step-by-step process for each type of stroke; a kind of guideline that takes into account the optimal mechanics for the "ideal" shot. Because of the nature of the game and the layout of the court, the padel technique strays slightly from that of tennis or squash. Even if it may look similar to its counter-parts, the footwork and stance adopted by the player, as well as the swing of the racquet, tend to be shorter and more swift. Likewise, since a paddle has no strings, the types of effects differ from those of other racquet sports. Indeed, much of the technique in padel has been adapted to aid its inherent strategic qualities (e.g., ball placement instead of powerful winners) whilst saving energy during the long rallies. And though movements are more stream-lined and require less physical effort from players, devel-oping a solid technique is akin to building the backbone of your game and provide the "arsenal" for following through with your tactics.

There are six prime strokes in padel and several variations thereof. In essence, any shot a player hits – besides those clumsy, rushed dives to save the ball at any cost – falls into one of these categories.

THE FOREHAND

As a rather intuitive movement and one of the groundstrokes, the forehand is the bread-and-butter shot of padel; the first technique any player will or should learn. The mechanics itself are straightforward: it consists of the natural reaction anyone would take if they had to swing at a ball coming toward them with the palm of their hand. Most people would automatically hit the ball with their dominant hand, stepping toward it with the opposite foot. That is why, when possible, most players choose to hit a forehand instead of a backhand. Obviously, a right-handed person will perform the forehand on the opposite side (turning to his/her right side) as a left-hander. But the technique is the same regardless of handedness.

In padel, the forehand is often seen as a placement shot, used primarily to defend and thus requiring more control than power. The movement can be broken down into three parts. Starting from the ready position, the first step is to bring the racquet back, turning your shoulders and hips with it so your torso is oriented laterally in relation to the ball. Then, move your feet to the same lateral position – often sideways to the court – in order to make the bodyweight transfer from back to front more easily. Finally, swing the racquet horizontally so it contacts the ball just in front of the hip, around waist-high, following through until just in front of your body. Many beginners make the mistake of not taking the racquet back at once; they move into position before setting up the racquet, which means having to rush the shot when the ball arrives. Or else they overlook or forget to do the footwork and lock a firm stance, using only their arms to carry out the shot instead of turning their body, stepping into the ball, and tapping into the bodyweight transition to promote drive and power.

THE BACKHAND

Stance-wise, the backhand is the opposite of the forehand. You swing at the ball with the back of your hand/racquet. Hence, right-handed players perform the backhand on their left side, whereas left-handers hit the backhand from their right side. It is precisely the orientation of the movement – having to bring the hand around the body – that makes the backhand less natural and less comfortable for many players. Nevertheless, one doesn't always have the option to choose which groundstroke to hit, so both are equally important. As with the forehand, the first step of the backhand is to bring the racquet behind one's body. This is often done by holding the throat of the racquet with the opposite hand to help guide the movement. Once the racquet is in place, get your feet into a position where shoulders and hips are both facing sideways, securing a stable and balanced stance. Again, the swing travels horizontally, and although both hands are on the racquet at the ready position, they release shortly after the move has started. The racquet contacts the ball near the waistline, just in front of the hip, and the move finishes slightly past the right side of the body with arms open.

When setting up for a backhand, beginners tend to bring the racquet high up to their shoulders and chop down the ball, as opposed to swinging the racquet horizontally and using the bodyweight transfer to push the ball forward. Needless to say, this kind of technique curbs power and control, often giving the ball too much spin. Another common error is not doing the footwork, stretching the arms and flicking the wrists to tap the ball instead of walking up to it and ensuring the contact is made in front of the hips.

Something unique about the backhand, and a motif for a lot of doubt and controversy, is whether to perform the move double-handed or single-handed. Watching World Padel Tour matches, you will notice that some players use a double-handed backhand for some shots and a single-handed for others. When choosing what works best for you, the first thing to acknowledge is that there is no problem with hitting a double-handed backhand. Many players and coaches are against it, but that doesn't change the fact that, for many people, it is physically much easier to hit the ball with two hands. Likewise, some padel players have a background in tennis, where double-handed backhands are very common, and thus find it easy to transition the technique to padel. As with tennis, the main objective of a double-handed backhand is to use the opposite hand to push through the ball and generate extra power. Therefore, even if a player doesn't fully adopt the double-handed technique, they might find it very useful when deep in the corner of the court, a situation where the other hand may assist in generating the power needed to hit the ball across strategically. Conversely, there are cases –

such as when the ball bounces off the glass and goes away from the player – where one can benefit greatly from a single-handed shot. Single-handed backhands provide more reach and flexibility than a double, emphasising control over power. That is why the majority of players end up opting for the single-handed technique – the game of padel doesn't require much power, and the power you need can usually be generated with one hand. Thus, adding another hand may only complicate the technique.

THE SERVE

Whilst services in padel don't play as crucial of a role as in tennis, a well-executed technique ensures an advantage when placing yourself in an attack position. Plus, as the stroke that initiates the point, players want to at least make it over the net and avoid a double fault. Especially for beginners, who often attempt a service beyond what their skills allow or try to hit the ball immediately off the rise, it is important to keep the move as simple as possible. The goal here is not to hit an ace, as in tennis; it is to achieve consistency and accuracy. And yet, despite its significance and how easy it is to practice, most people don't give enough attention to their serve.

The ready position for a service is the same as that of a forehand. Feet stand apart, facing the side walls in a solid stance with knees slightly flexed; the racquet is held behind the body a little further up, so as to come down on the ball in a sort of pendulum motion. The opposite arm holds the ball at shoulder height, dropping it just in front of the front foot towards the court. Once the ball touches the ground, the racquet should swing through and hit it at about waist height

– and that is all there is to it. When players have mastered the momentum of the bounce-and-swing, they can start employing their own body momentum in the court more actively. For that, you start by leaning on the back foot, dropping the ball, and rocking forward as you contact the ball. In fact, this is quite a natural move, since most players would come up to the net right after the service.

It is very common for beginners to hit an aggressive first serve and, failing at it, play an extra-safe second serve, simply pushing the ball into the opponent's court. Needless to say, this will make it easier for the returner to assume an offensive stance, so the advantage the server could gain is lost. Therefore, when starting to practice your serve, try to develop two equally consistent shots, both of which could be relied upon tactically. Another typical mistake among those starting out is to rush to the net before the stroke is complete. This hurried technique will have direct consequences on serve placement, often driving it willy-nilly as opposed to strategic positions that would cause problems to the returner. So, keep in mind: swing the racquet, make contact, finish the movement – then sprint to the net.

THE LOB

The lob is a high shot that takes the ball in an arching trajectory over your opponents; it is a variation of the groundstroke and can be performed either with a forehand or a backhand. Usually played by those defending, the lob is also considered one of the most defining shots in padel. It can dramatically switch the dynamic of a point, e.g., by pushing the opponents to the back of their court into a defensive position, and moving forward to the net to take over the offensive – which is precisely the aim of padel. Moreover, because the lob is a slow shot, it also helps in changing the pace of the point, allowing defence players to catch a breath and regroup. In other words, it is as indispensable to any player's arsenal as the service.

Speaking of technique, the starting position for a lob is pretty much the same as any other shot: racquet back, body turned sideways in relation to the ball, feet in a well-balanced stance. The difference is subtle but significant: players should flex their knees more than usual, assuming an extra-low posture whence to hit the ball from below, and finish the move with the racquet higher up. These slightly distinct mechanics influence how high and deep the lob will go, and consequently, how effective it will be in pushing your opponents backwards. Many players don't set themselves up properly and execute the lob when they are off-balance. This minor error can be fatal, as it will result in a bad lob, and a bad lob is a great opportunity for your adversaries to respond with an aggressive attack. Similarly, some players get into the habit of lifting their entire body to the point of almost jumping, in the hope that this added heave will increase the ball's height. More often than not, however, it makes them lose balance, hindering the direction of the shot – and the aim just so happens to be the most important factor in the lob. Players should strive to hit high lobs that get the ball in the deep corner of the court, past the service line. In such scenarios, the ball bounces and remains close to the back wall, thus putting the opponent in a tricky position. A faster and lower lob, on the other hand, will bounce and spring off the back wall, giving the opponent more space and time to prepare for a return.

THE VOLLEY

Another fundamental technique in padel is the volley. This kind of stroke is executed mostly by players on the offensive as a means to pressure the opponent and destabilise their game. The movement itself resembles a quick punch with the racquet, struck with almost no backswing. Essentially, every shot taken prior to the ball touching the ground is a volley – apart from the smash and its variations. Hence, volleys can be performed either on the backhand or the forehand, and are mainly used when players are near the net.

When setting up for a volley, players should face the net and hold their racquet slightly further from their body in a vertical position. The feet should stand apart with the knees somewhat bent, planting a solid stance. Usually, the non-dominant hand holds the throat of the racquet to help with stability. By orientating their body thus, players are faster to react when the ball approaches. And, since they stand closer to the net (and to their opponent), the ball will take less time to reach their racquet, which makes reflex all-important.

Although the movement is shorter than that of a forehand or a backhand, players should still take their racquet back (as far as their back shoulder) to perform a volley, turning their front shoulder toward the net. Next, they should step forward toward the ball with the opposite leg from their dominant hand. For instance, a right-handed player hitting a volley on their forehand would step forward with their left leg. This part of the move is essential, as it establishes a stable base for the stroke and ensures one's body weight is transferred to the shot. Lastly, the racquet should contact the ball just in front of the body, more as a block than a swing, with the wrist and forearm locked firmly. Keeping the technique simple allows the racquet to harness the power coming from the opponent's shot and merely rebound it back onto their court. Backhand volleys are performed in exactly the same way, only requiring the wrist and forearm to stand even more firmly so the racquet doesn't wobble upon contact. Regardless of the side, when executing lower volleys, players should bend their knees (not their hips) and get down closer to the ground whilst keeping the racquet head in an upward position. This small detail is frequently overlooked by beginners, who end up dropping the head of the racquet down and flicking the ball with a motion of the wrist, which results in a feeble shot lacking control.

Because the mechanics of a volley are slightly different from those of a groundstroke, players often feel they have to reposition the racquet in their hands. They tend to alter the grip so the hitting surface faces their body and leave their hips and shoulder open, performing the movement in a patting motion as opposed to a block. Yet this drastically hinders the effectiveness of the volley. Therefore, keeping a continental grip and making sure the shoulders turn sideways when stepping toward the net is of the essence when achieving a solid, controlled block.

Besides the technique itself, beginners seldom position themselves properly for a volley. They usually come up very close to the net, attempting to pat the ball down into the opponent's court. Consequently, that leaves a lot of open space behind their backs, making it easier for the adversaries.

It also shortens the distance between them and their opponents, meaning they will have less time to react to the ball. That is why those just starting out should get used to standing roughly two metres away from the net. Such distance allows players to move forward to hit shorter volleys but also cover the back of the court, lessening the chances of being lobbed and improving the positioning for a smash.

THE SMASH

The smash is the main type of overhead shot played in response to a lob. Its primary objective is to either finish the point or buy time to get back to the net. To execute a smash, players bring the racquet back, slightly above shoulder height, with the head pointing upwards. As with groundstrokes – or any other shot, for that matter – it is important to assume a lateral position in relation to the ball, doing the necessary footwork to place oneself just below where the ball is supposed to land. An action specific to smashes is the raising of the front arm, pointing up to the ball and following its movement. Not only is this helpful to establish a sense of positioning and timing, but also to keep both shoulders up during preparation and thus employ a downward motion upon contact.

Unlike in tennis, where smashes are rare, padel players hit an average of two to three smashes per rally. Also, whereas tennis smashes are always aggressive, padel smashes vary between offensive and defensive depending on several factors. The first thing a player should consider when hitting a smash is their position on the court. Standing toward the front section of the court allows for a more aggressive approach, but if the lob has forced the player to move further back, a defensive variation is more suitable for being able to regain the net position. Taking the height of the lob into account also affects the decision of which kind of smash to hit. High lobs are particularly tricky to attack. In such instances, players may find it easier to use a more conservative variation, such as the bandeja. Conversely, a low-to-medium high lob favours a more flat and powerful stroke.

A common mistake when performing a smash – especially for those who have transitioned from tennis – is to disregard one's own position and always try to use a lot of power. A badly executed smash, say, when one loses balance whilst stepping back, will likely result in an easy shot for the opponent to counter-attack. Therefore, when in an unfavourable position and/or stance, players should opt for one of the two most common variations of the smash – the bandeja and the vibora. Technique-wise, both strokes differ slightly from the standard flat smash. They contact the outside of the ball at head-height, adding some (or lots) of slice effect to drag the ball down upon bouncing on the opponent's court.

Usually played further back in the court, the bandeja can be seen as a defensive variation of the smash. It aims to gain time to reclaim the net position. This is done by directing the ball into one of the corners of the opponent's court (as opposed to hitting the ball aggressively), forcing them into a difficult defensive situation. The vibora, on the other hand, has a more offensive quality to it. It is performed closer to the net and often aims to force the opponent to commit an error. Instead of relying on power, the vibora uses a faster racquet head-speed to create a slice effect and put the opponent in a position where their response is highly compromised.

THE BACK GLASS

The back glass is a highly useful, defensive shot – a variation of the groundstrokes. It is normally taken after a player has been lobbed and compelled to sprint to the back of the court to rescue the ball. Although it cannot be used as a means to attack, playing off the back glass/wall may be a good opportunity to hit the ball in a direction or with a particular effect that will make the response more difficult. And since the walls are an integral – and unavoidable – part of padel, no match is won without employing such a technique. Hence, getting comfortable with using them for one's benefit is imperative. As a rule of thumb, any shot that bounces on or behind your service line should be left to hit off the back wall.

In terms of technique, the back glass doesn't differ much from the forehand or the backhand. Indeed, the mechanics at the start are the same: take the racquet back and turn the torso to a sideways position in relation to the ball. The difference begins with the footwork. Players should move back in line with the ball, following it forward as it bounces off the glass and making contact just in front of the body – as with the groundstrokes. Inexperienced players often make the mistake of not moving back with the ball. They have the habit of staying planted, waiting for the ball to bounce back. But this causes them to make contact in all sorts of awkward positions, which, in turn, limits their options on ball placement and effects. Conversely, following the ball and hitting in front of their bodies means they can choose between a lob or low shot to force the opponent's error, for instance. Likewise, it is not uncommon for players to forget to move forward with the ball once it comes off the wall. When this happens, the entire technique is compromised. They no longer make contact in a comfortable position and instead have to stretch their arms to merely slap the ball.

Playing off the back glass is relatively straightforward when the ball comes in a straight line – it will bounce back in almost the same direction whence it came. However, when hit at an angle, the ball will probably also come off the wall at an angle, thus requiring players to adjust accordingly and "read" the ball more carefully. A lot of it comes down to experience and the intuitive knowledge gathered from hitting this kind of oblique shot, but it is also a mathematical issue that concerns the angle of entry and exit. Hence, making a rough prediction of where the ball is going to travel after contacting the wall can inform which position to take for the stroke. By following the course of the incoming shot and keeping a comfortable space between their bodies and the ball, players can then perform the technique as usual. In such instances, it is better to allow more space between the body and the ball and move toward it to take the shot than to be far too close and execute the stroke hurriedly.

EFFECTS

While general mechanics and court positioning define the type of shot a player hits, the fashion in which the racquet comes in contact with the ball defines the effect it produces. And though effects may seem like a mere detail in execution, they have a direct impact on how the ball lands on the opponent's court and, consequently, how they return the shot. As such, the same kind of stroke (e.g., a forehand) can assume distinct characteristics according to the effect employed.

FLAT

For most people, flat strokes are the natural way to hit a ball. Because it is easy to execute and provides good control in terms of power and direction, it is always the first type of effect to master in padel. For a flat stroke, players have to ensure the racquet is perpendicular to the ground upon contacting the ball. The movement itself travels forward in a straight line, hitting the ball from behind. Smashes, volleys, off-the-glass shots, and weak balls near the net are the most common instances in which to employ the flat effect. As a downside, the bounce of a flat stroke is easy to predict and often comes at a height that makes it easier to return.

BACKSPIN/SLICE

A backspin or slice effect entails hitting the lower half of the ball with an angled, downward motion, finishing up the movement slightly ahead of the body and above the point of contact. It can be executed in groundstrokes as well as volleys, and in certain instances, as the vibora variation of the smash – the latter utilising a somewhat different, attack-oriented technique. As the name suggests, the technique is very much about slicing or brushing the ball, not so much about pushing it forward. It is this swift motion of the racquet that adds extra spin to the ball, making it bounce irregularly upon landing on the other side of the court. Slice shots are particularly useful when the opponent is at the back of the court or in a relatively unfavourable volleying position. They are not as fast or easy to direct as flat or topspin effects, so the use of slices is often left to the service, volleys, and approaches.

TOPSPIN

The topspin – the most-used effect in tennis – consists of hitting the top section of the ball in an upward and forward motion. It is similar to the backspin in that it merely brushes the ball instead of striking it head-on. However, the action is performed inversely and the ball travels in a parabola instead of a straight line. A major upside of this type of effect is the speed it generates. This speed, in turn, causes the ball to bounce higher and faster upon landing on the opponent's court, disturbing their response. Whilst these factors can be advantageous, if badly executed, the topspin effect may well make things easier for the adversary. This is often the case when a topspin ball bounces off the back wall; it tends to come up high, which gives the opponent time to set up a good shot.

COMMON BEGINNER ERRORS

Part of the stimulation behind any kind of sport is the challenge – and reward – of learning with one's mistakes. In that sense, padel is no different: the more one practices, the better one gets. Yet, those starting out don't have years of experience to fall back on, and sometimes have no proper guidance to help them identify where they are erring and thereby shorten the learning curve. At the same time, people coming from other racquet sports such as squash or tennis benefit from understanding how to manipulate a racquet, how to do the footwork and get into position, or how to strike a forehand, but they still have to adjust to the pace and equipment of padel, as well as the idea of always playing with a partner in the layout of the court. In fact, it is not uncommon for a good habit developed in tennis to become a bad habit in padel. So, when taking the first steps into the world of padel, it is important to observe certain aspects of one's game; frequent mistakes, beyond technique, which can become a stone in one's shoe, so to speak.

STICKING TO ONE GRIP

As previously mentioned, the grip is an oft-overlooked element of padel. Most people wouldn't mull it over too much, so long as the racquet feels comfortable and stable in their hand. However, since it has implications both on technique and the health of a player's arm, the grip should be at the forefront of every beginner's mind. Hence, whether you have played tennis before or are holding a racquet for the first time, getting used to the continental grip (the most common hand position in padel) as soon as possible will mean completing the first milestone successfully – and for good.

IMPROVING COORDINATION

Though each player has their own level of coordination, failing to give it due attention from the get-go is one of the main issues among beginners. In padel, coordination is specifically related to setting yourself in the right position (in relation to the ball), performing the technique with the right tempo, and hitting the ball at the right time. It also has to do with reading the trajectory and speed of the ball, predicting the shot, and planning accordingly. After all, failing to do so often results in hitting the ball clumsily and far away from the ideal point of contact. Fortunately, like any skill, coordination can be worked on and improved, and a good level of coordination ensures your strokes drive the ball with the power and direction you wish.

MAKING USE OF COURT POSITIONING

Also highlighted previously, court positioning is a basic concept of padel that is often underestimated by those starting out. Indeed, the way a player moves around the court and how well they make use of attack-defence dynamics is a major difference between beginners and experts. Initiates tend to stay at the back of the court and hit all shots from behind the service line, as though afraid of coming up to the net. And whilst net game can be intimidating at times, it is also the most effective way to score points in padel. Hence, developing early confidence to move according to situations and opportunities is the best way to ensure your ability to position on the court becomes an ally rather than a hindrance.

KEEPING THE FEET WORKING

Footwork is an underlying factor that influences all physical aspects in padel – including coordination and court positioning. It is safe to say that, when learning the technique, most beginners pay attention to their upper-body movement – not their lower body. Yet, how well a player sets their feet into position has a direct impact on the way the shot will be taken, and consequently, the power, direction, and effect on the ball. Moreover, active footwork ensures the player is always ready to react, switching position and starting for the ball as/when necessary.

BENDING THE KNEES

Another lower-body activity that plays a crucial role in performance (and avoiding injuries) is knee flex. Watching beginners play, one can usually spot three out of the four players failing to bend their knees when executing strokes. The first downside of a stiff-legged posture is that the body-weight transfer necessary for driving the ball forward during shots becomes much more difficult and less effective. Another issue relates to low balls. Players who don't flex their knees end up bending their backs to reach the ball, which disrupts the entire technique, thus compromising the shot itself. Finally, and perhaps more importantly, ensuring an active flex of the knees helps to cushion the impact when sprinting, halting, or jumping during rallies.

TEAMWORK MAKES IT WORK

Given the format of a padel match, it is impossible to disregard the fact that you are not alone. This may be particularly relevant to those transitioning from squash or tennis, where the individual mindset is the norm. Such synergy is, therefore, a decisive factor in any padel team, and making sure you and your partner work together not only tactically but also emotionally (through support and motivation) is crucial. That is why, whether competing or only enjoying a friendly game, players should exercise a team approach right from the start. Once you are in harmony with your partner, decisions become almost second nature, movements on the court more fluid, and the match more fun.

LEARNING PADEL

Different people learn in different ways. Some prefer a guided, highly didactic approach, while others thrive on learning-by-doing, progressing faster when left to figure things out by themselves. The same applies to padel: one has to identify the best learning method(s) for their personality and purpose.

In padel, unlike football, for example, technique often overshadows talent. That is why professional padel players and coaches will generally stand by a particular, designed way of performing – especially in terms of stroke technique. But the fact remains that if a player doesn't feel comfortable, chances are their game will neither flow nor improve. Therefore, beginners should always remember that guidelines are there with the objective of guiding – not restricting. That said, there are huge advantages in taking lessons and having someone point out flaws and give tips to develop your skills.

Perhaps the most important benefit to taking lessons is the opportunity to follow a training methodology to direct and optimise one's learning curve. These ecosystems of development are often broken down per genre, and end up entwining with each other depending on the coach's assessment for a particular player or class. Generally, all training methodologies will encompass physical, technical, mental, and strategic sections.

• Physical: Developing coordination and motor skills with a specific focus on speed and agility, and the strengthening of muscles for endurance and balance.

• Technical: Looking step-by-step at the elements of a padel game, such as court positioning and movement, different types of strokes and effects, and attack-and-defence dynamics.

• Mental: Working on pressure and stress management, building confidence, setting goals, exercising concentration and determination, and establishing a positive mentality toward the game and a respectful attitude toward the team.

• Strategy: Learning the theoretical ins-and-outs of padel and how to develop a tactical view of the game based on personal strengths and interpersonal communication with the partner.

Much like every padel academy and/or coach will have their own methodology, they will also assess a player's skill level in order to determine what type of training to carry out. Although there is no such thing as an "official padel level chart", it is possible to have an idea of where a player stands proficiency-wise by looking at their overall playing experience and their current stage in technique development. Some padel academies adopt a marking system (from 1 to 7, for example) to measure a player's skill level according to their achievements. In the end, however, categorising one's ability serves more to give an idea of one's learning curve and determining which training programme to enrol in than stipulating whether or not they are apt to play this or that match.

Those who approach schools or coaches intending to play padel at an amateur level will often have their skills assessed as such:

• A1: Also known as Initiation, the A1 level represents the very first stage in padel, where players have little to no knowledge of the game and technique. Level A1 classes will usually introduce a player to the very basics of padel, e.g. basic game terminology, parts of the court, rules of play, how to hold a racquet, fundamental strokes, etc. After completing this level, players are able to join beginner-level matches.

• A2: Level A2 generally focuses on solidifying the basic knowledge acquired on A1 and building the player's confidence. This is done by introducing drill exercises that simulate the different situations in which a player may hit the same stroke, thus honing their technique and giving them a better understanding of game dynamics. Technical analysis and correction of movements is a big part of this stage. It is also at this level that players begin to familiarise themselves with playing off the walls. A2 is sometimes seen as the first step toward an intermediate status.

• B1: As a transition level, B1 classes revolve around boosting the efficiency of already-known techniques and working on most common mistakes. It is assumed that, at this stage, players feel comfortable moving around the court and executing all fundamental strokes. Getting acquainted with effects and special shots, such as the bandeja, the vibora, half-volleys, and drop shots, is also part of the B1 curriculum. Coaches tend to assign more complex and intense drills, challenging learners to start thinking tactically and consider real-life situations. After B1, players should have a solid base of the game and are able to join higher-level games without being left behind.

• C1: The C1 level is tantamount to the advanced status, and much of the structure of this stage is directed at competition or competition simulations. This means learning to deal with pressure, improving teamwork, and playing lots of best-of-three-sets matches. Players who have reached C1 will be familiar with all padel techniques, will have been initiated in tactics and strategy, and will begin to dive further into the mental aspects of the game. The on-court practice is much more intense and deals with improving the execution of stroke variations. C1 trainees who wish to participate in tournaments will often prepare for events under a well-structured training plan that comprises physical and theoretical practices as well as dietary follow-ups. This professionally-oriented approach looks at identifying the player's strong points and designing a game pattern. Henceforth, classes begin to take the shape of holistic, athletic training more than an instructional session.

PREVENTING INJURIES

Whilst padel presents a lot of physical benefits to those who practice it regularly (e.g., improves coordination and cardio-vascular activity, strengthens the musculature, lowers choles-terol, etc.), it also bears the threat of potential injuries. When playing an all-around sport such as padel that works both upper and lower body parts, any area or muscle is vulnerable to overexertion. And, like tennis, the fact that muscles are engaged asymmetrically means that spot overload occurs constantly. Thus, compensation exercises are of the essence.

Fortunately, most minor injuries – such as cramps, sprains, shin splints, and pulled muscles – can be prevented by wearing adequate gear, warming up and stretching before and after practice, and ensuring your overall fitness lives up to the physical effort undertaken. Others, like blisters or sunburns, can be taken care of with over-the-counter medication. Indeed, most people will feel discomfort here and there when playing padel – it is part of being an athlete. But some players, especially those who suffer from chronic pains or tend to spend extended periods of time at the padel court, are more susceptible to experiencing more serious types of injuries, which may require medical care. Of these graver traumas, the most common among padel players are tendinitis, tennis elbow, and joint pains, particularly around knees, shoulders, and ankles.

The first thing to do when sustaining an injury is to assess its severity and whether it requires medical attention. If a particular area has remained swollen or reddened for more than a day, or if a bruise has appeared without having bumped into an object, it is advisable to get it checked up. Likewise, a doctor should be consulted if/when a mild, steady pain (e.g., chest pains or muscular pangs) hinders your ability to play and doesn't go away after a day. On any other occasion, such as discomforts or slight swellings, the usual RICE (Rest, Ice, Compress, Elevate) technique can do much to curb and cure it.

Besides prevention methods and treatments, making sure that the body is constantly replenished with fluids helps to fight off injuries. After all, dehydration is one of the main underlying causes of cramps and muscular fatigue, which then lead to tissue damage. Studies on adequate hydration recommend at least 8 cups of fluid (water or juice, no alcoholic or caffeinated beverages) before playing and a minimum of 8 ounces/250ml every 20 minutes during practice. That said, it is always better to be on the safe side and "over-hydrate" oneself, even if not thirsty. But when considering injuries, perhaps the most important factor of all is understanding one's limitations and developing a well-balanced padel routine. This entails keeping in shape physically, listening to one's body, and following a regular schedule that gives the body time to rest and recuperate.

PEOPLE MAKE padel what it is. And whilst a love for the sport is one of the things that unites players, each person has a different "padel story" to tell.

In this chapter, we feature a Q&A with padel players

from across the globe who share tips, insights, and hopes for the sport.

———

ANTONIO JOSÉ PALACIOS ÁLVAREZ

Antonio José Palacios Álvarez is a 35-year-old amateur padel player from Malaga, Spain. He is founder of Padel Addict, an online publication dedicated to all things-padel – from news to tips and equipment reviews.

– *How and when did you start playing padel?*

– I started playing padel in 2008, but I discovered the sport even before that. I remember playing 1×1 in a normal court (instead of 2×2). There were already many padel courts in Malaga at that time, so I was aware that the sport existed. But it was only when a tennis partner of mine and I started playing friendly matches – and, a little bit later, tournaments – that I fell in love with this beautiful sport. I have been playing since then.

– *Where and with whom do you usually play?*

– When you have been playing for so long, you make a lot of "padel friends." I usually play with teammates or players from other teams. I also play in an amateur tournament called SNP.

– *What is it that attracts you to padel?*

– Well, it's pure enjoyment! Padel is very fun and competitive at the same time. At the beginning, you don't need too much technique; it is easy to improve. It is easy to witness progress after only playing for a few months. Moreover, it is a very social sport.

— *In what ways has padel changed your life?*

— I have made many new friends and have lived great experiences with teammates, winning some tournaments. In addition, it has helped me to keep fit.

— *What are the main challenges you have faced when playing padel?*

— The main challenge is to get better results and improve your level of play. This is particularly the case in tournaments, where playing finals or qualifying matches that will take the team to the next round can be extra challenging. But when you win these matches, you feel like you have really overcome something. You feel like the best guy in the world!

— *What tip(s) would you give to anyone starting out at padel?*

— Mainly to enjoy the game. Be patient and try to learn the rules. I would also recommend buying good equipment to play. And if you don't know any padel players, you can just ask at your local padel clubs. They usually organise matches between beginners. Once you start playing, you won't regret it!

— *How do you see the sport growing in the future?*

— Over the last few years, padel has been growing incredibly fast in other countries besides Spain. Sweden is a great example. Nowadays, you can find padel courts in almost any country on every continent. I strongly believe that Padel is going to keep growing more and more. And maybe, in a few years, Padel could be an Olympic sport – why not?

RAQUEL PILTCHER

Raquel Piltcher is a 29-year-old professional padel player from Pelotas, Brazil. She is currently number 32 in the World Padel Tour ranking and has been living in Madrid, Spain, since 2017.

– *How did you find out about padel? And when did you start playing?*

– I first heard about padel when I was 7 years old. There was a big padel boom in the south of Brazil, and many clubs started sprouting. Soon the trend abated and I started to play tennis. I dedicated myself to a career in professional tennis until I was 22 years old. After quitting tennis, I moved back over to padel – and I was hooked.

– *What makes padel special for you?*

– I love how dynamic the sport is and how easy it is for anyone to learn and have fun right from the start. Coming from tennis, I know how difficult it can be for a beginner to start playing and how long it takes before one is able to play well enough to have fun. With padel, it is different. Since it is so easy to pick up, in little time beginners are already having lots of fun.

– *In your opinion, besides the court, equipment, and rules, what makes padel different from tennis?*

– I think padel is more fun; it has a sort of magic to it. Because it has so many different techniques and tactics, it provides more of a spectacle than tennis.

– *How has padel impacted your life?*

– Padel has given me the opportunity to live off a sport, to experience life in a different country, and to dedicate my work to something that I truly enjoy – competing.

– *What is the main challenge you face in padel?*

– I think it is to change my conception of the fact that I can do something that I love, something vocational, and chase that idea. Also, to continuously believe that I can make daily changes in myself to a better player and person.

– *What tips would you give to someone who is getting started in padel?*

– Have fun! Simply enjoy your time in the padel court.

– *What are your thoughts on the future of padel?*

– I see that each year padel takes a step forward, a new country is integrated. There is a lot of work happening to take the sport further than Spain, and I think that is the way to go. We are still a relatively small tribe, but little by little, more people are becoming interested in padel. I hope that soon we are able to reach a large enough number of players to make it into the Olympics. That would be a dream come true.

LUCAS SACHELLO

Lucas Sachello is a 28-year-old amateur padel player from Buenos Aires, Argentina.

– *How did you get into padel?*

– I have known about padel ever since I was a kid. The sport underwent a boom in Argentina during the 80s and 90s; courts could be found everywhere, and tournaments were aired in public TV channels. I used to play with high school friends, but very seldom. In 2013, some of my friends and I formed a padel group and played often for around one year. I injured my left leg and ankle quite badly while playing football, so after recovering in July, 2019, I made a full transition into padel and have been playing regularly ever since.

— *Where and with whom do you usually play?*

— At first, I always played with friends or co-workers. Now that I'm more into it, I'm playing tournaments and asking local clubs to arrange matches. I usually play at local clubs, 1-2 days per week.

— *What do you like the most about padel?*

— One of the things I like the most is that it doesn't have an age-cap (in some sports, you start declining after reaching your 30s). And although it's more active than tennis, it's also very beginner-friendly. I love sports, and I've played everything from football to rugby, volley, basketball, and tennis. With padel, I was able to continue pursuing my passion after the injury without feeling handicapped at all.

— *In what ways has padel impacted your life?*

— It has allowed me to practice sports consistently again whilst enjoying a friendly environment, getting competitive, and making friends along the way.

— *What challenges do you face when playing padel?*

— I think the challenge has been the same as with any sport: the determination and time you need to improve your skills. I'm very self-critical by nature, constantly looking for ways to evolve. And in padel, there is always a lot of room for improvement.

— *What tip(s) would you give to anyone starting out at padel?*

— At first, just enjoy yourself. Try to form a group of friends and/or go to a club and start hanging out there. Just see if you like it or not, regardless of how good you are. If you realize you like it, the best way to improve is to take classes and watch videos online. Even if you play every day, you're likely to keep making the same mistakes – unless you have a coach to watch and correct you. You can get better by playing every day, but the quirks that you develop will be hard to get rid of once you get used to them.

– *How do you see padel growing in Argentina in the future?*

– I think padel is getting a lot of traction lately. World Padel Tour is getting bigger each day, even after the pandemic hiatus. There are a lot of great new players and the sport seems to be booming in many places in Europe, particularly Portugal, Sweden, and Italy. South America is undergoing another surge. In Argentina, padel boomed in the 80s and 90s. After the recession, new opportunities arose in Spain. Still, we have produced some of the best players in the world and have been keeping our courts fresh with new talent. Since 2018, padel started growing again. Tournaments are happening more often and it's hard to book courts from 5-6 pm until 11 pm. You also see many people posting about padel in social media. I think the next 5 years are going to be pretty amazing.

FRANCESC CRUZ

Francesc Cruz is a 28-year-old amateur padel player from Barcelona, Spain.

– *What was your first contact with padel?*

–I started playing padel in 2012 whilst taking a law degree at the University of Barcelona. One of my best friends was the son of a tennis instructor; it was he who introduced me to padel. We used to get a free padel match every week at his father's academy. That's how I got to know the game. Back then, it was already starting to become popular – but nothing compared to what it is now in Spain.

– *Where and with whom do you usually play?*

– I used to play padel with my colleagues from university. When I started working, I lost touch with them and began playing padel with my co-workers. I felt lucky to work in a firm where so many people played padel. But then I realized that padel had exploded in Spain – everybody was playing it. Nowadays, I play at the tennis-padel club near my house in the suburbs of Barcelona. The facility has 4 tennis courts and 6 padel courts, 2 of which are outdoors. That said, there are more than 10 padel clubs in a 15-kilometre radius from where I live. I play with people from the club, co-workers, friends, my partner, my sister, and my family. My brother-in-law is currently my padel partner in amateur tournaments.

– *What are your favourite things about padel?*

– Padel is really easy to pick up. It's not very physically demanding and is suitable for all ages. But what I like the most is that it is a social sport. You meet a lot of people and create bonds with everyone you play with. One of my friends says that padel is not worth the physical effort because he always ends up having beers after the game and all calories burned are regained in 5 minutes. Another plus of padel is that it is easy to find people to play with. Finally, the feeling you get when hitting a perfect volley, a great bandeja to the corner, or smashing the ball outside the court is really satisfying.

– *How has padel improved your life?*

– That I have to run, jump, crouch, duck, and hit many

times in the span of a point has helped me connect with my body. But also, as with tennis, padel has an important psychological component. You can't let your mind get distracted, since the tiniest mistake can cost a point. You have to keep your mind in the moment, in the point, in the ball, and in the way you are going to hit it. That is one of the lessons that padel has taught me: Keep your mind here and now, forget about yesterday, try not to think of tomorrow – just hit the ball as well as you can. Moreover, you have to help your partner stay focused as well. Many are the matches when a team loses because of inexistent communication or a lack of support between partners. This another lesson padel has taught me: by helping your partner feel good and improve, you are helping yourself.

– *What sort of challenges do you face when playing padel?*

– For me, one of the trickiest part of padel is returning those nasty spin balls to the corner. You have to predict the trajectory of the ball, move, let it pass, duck, prepare the stroke, wait, and hit the ball once you have enough space for the movement – but just before the ball bounces for second time. And even when you manage to return them, your shot usually proves really easy for the opponent to smash. Another challenging aspect for me are the bandeja and the vibora. These shots doesn't exist in tennis and are really hard to master. Something I struggled with at the beginning was understanding that I have to predict the trajectory of the lob and position myself behind the ball so as to hit it when it is in front of me. That means you have to be faster with your legs.

– *What tip(s) would you give to anyone starting out at padel?*

– First of all, if you are starting with padel, know that you have made a great decision by letting this sport into your life. You are going to learn new things, have fun, and meet lots of different people. Besides the technical aspects, my advice would be to remember that padel is a sport that requires companionship. Treat your partner with respect, always be kind and supportive. Also, don't be afraid to ask questions of those more experienced and don't be afraid to try new shots in a game.

As one of my friends says: There are two mistakes you can make in padel. The first is considering yourself a better player than you actually are. If this happens, whether you hit the ball to the glass or the net, you are going to disappoint yourself, and that will make your game worse. The second is considering yourself worse than you actually are. If this happens, you are always going to be afraid to try new things lest you miss the shot. So always try to be aware of your level. Finally, don't underestimate the importance of padel lessons. A good teacher will help you a lot in improving your game.

– How has padel been growing in Barcelona? And how do you see it developing in the future?

– Padel used to be considered a posh sport in Barcelona. It was mainly played by rich people who were getting too old for tennis but wanted to keep playing a racquet sport, and who could afford to join a club that happened to have padel courts. In the late 90s, padel became more popular after one of Spain's ex-presidents (José María Aznar) mentioned that he was playing padel on a weekly basis. So it's funny to think how a once-elitist sport is now one of the most-played sports in the country.

This boom was also promoted by entrepreneurs who saw a business opportunity in padel and started opening low-cost clubs in major Spanish cities. The fact that Spain benefits from fair weather year-round has helped the building of outdoors padel clubs, which are cheaper to build and therefore cheaper to play at. For instance, the other day I rented a court for one and a half hours in a nearby city to play with some friends and it only cost us €3,50 per person.

During lockdown, all padel clubs had to close due to COVID-19. When they reopened, my friends and I struggled to find an available court to play on, even though there are plenty of padel clubs in Catalonia. We once had to drive for 30 km to play after calling more than 15 clubs with a week's notice! This shows that padel is in a very strong position in Spain. Parents used to enrol kids in tennis academies; now they play padel. And the fact that more people start playing from a very young age creates competition, which means better players in the future.

Padel has been helping people to get back in sport, work out, and spend quality time with friends and family. I love when my partner and I get home tired after a hard match and talk to each other about it and how are we improving. However, one thing that still surprises me is that, despite its popularity, not many people follow pro padel tournaments and the World Padel Tour. I think this is the next evolution in padel in Spain. We are also seeing other European countries getting into padel. Who knows, maybe one day we will see a French Padel Open or Padel version of Wimbledon in London. Or perhaps padel could become an Olympic sport? I can't wait to see what comes.

PAULO BASTOS

Paulo Bastos is a 39-year-old entrepreneur from Lisbon, Portugal. He's an amateur padel player and one of the many members the group Super GT Padel.

— *When did you start playing padel?*

— I started playing padel 2 years ago. I had never heard of it before, but someone from my family invited me and other family members for a casual game. We all got instantly hooked and have been playing non-stop since then, making padel part of our lives.

— *Where and with whom do you usually play?*

— We usually play from among our group of social players. Some are family members and others are friends that we have met while playing. This group has since grown quite a bit, and besides the casual games, we often organise amateur social tournaments. We also often participate in events from specific padel clubs or national tournaments for casual players. None of us play in official tournaments (yet), since that would be for more professional players on a higher level.

There are several padel clubs in Lisbon where we play, from big, professional clubs to smaller, neighbourhood clubs where everyone gets together as one big family of padel lovers. At the moment, the demand for padel is so big in Portugal that we just play wherever we are able to book a court – no chance to be picky with the preferred club.

— *What makes padel special for you?*

— I see padel as a mix of tennis and squash, with a good balance between the needs of the game versus the fun that you get from playing. Although there is a lot of technique and strategy that you can learn as you improve, the reality is that anyone can play padel, regardless of skill level, build, or age. The same is not really true for the more demanding sports such as tennis and squash. The strategy part of padel is what makes it more special for me. Once you improve on technique, the game evolves to something like chess, where you apply strategies and quick thinking to gain points and win the match.

– *In what ways has padel improved your life?*

– Padel is a very social sport and it has allowed me to meet lots of interesting people from all walks of life, some of whom are now my friends. Family members whom I seldom saw, old friends I had lost touch with – all of them are now part of the weekly padel meetings and the events that happen before and after the matches. Even my wife and kids now play padel and take up lessons. It's like a family love affair with padel.

– *What challenges do you face when playing padel?*

– Finding the time to play or take lessons whilst balancing it with the rest of your life can be a challenge. Besides, the current lack of courts available to book makes it more challenging since you can't simply grab your racquet and go play a game. If you are okay with just playing from time to time and have fun, it is not an issue. But if you have the desire to improve and maybe move up to the level above, you need to find the time to train.

– *What tip(s) would you give to anyone starting out at padel?*

– If you are starting, just have fun. Do not worry about anything, don't overthink it, and do not try to be like Paquito Navarro. If you love it and are interested in being a better player, find a cool padel club and take some lessons – it will make a big difference in your playing and help you avoid injuries.

– How is the padel scene in Portugal? And how do you see the sport growing in the future?

– In the past two years, there has been an explosive growth of padel in Portugal – and it doesn't look like this will stop. You used to be able to find a court to play anytime, but now, due to the demand, most clubs are fully booked. Even with a surge of new clubs, it doesn't seem enough. So I expect more new clubs to crop up in the future. There has also been an increase in social tournaments – from local to nationwide events as well as professional tournaments. The level of players is also increasing, and you can now find some Portuguese players in the WPT. Some stores specific to padel equipment have appeared and you can nowadays see the big sporting goods stores selling padel products as well, which wasn't the case before.

Although padel is growing strong, it is not yet a mainstream sport like tennis. But this can change, and in about five years, padel in Portugal might have clubs in every neighbourhood. Our geographical proximity to Spain (the Mecca of padel) can certainly be an advantage to the adoption and professionalization of padel in Portugal. At the moment, there is only one WPT event in Portugal each year, so I would love to see more elite-level tournaments happening here and maybe one day have a couple of top-seeded Portuguese players winning tournaments in the WPT.

OVER THE LAST DECADE, padel has asserted itself and claimed a position among the world's fastest-growing sports. Current estimates show there are around 8 million padel players around the world, with an average of 250 thousand new players getting started every year. From 2017 to 2018, there was a 40% increase in World Padel Tour match broadcasts and streams. Racquet sales soared from 83 thousand in 2002 to over 400 thousand in 2017. In Spain in 2019, the number of federated padel players surpassed that of tennis – a historic achievement. Granted, when looking at general statistics, padel cannot compare with mainstream sports such as football, which boasts roughly 265 million enthusiasts. But for a sport that is not even 100 years old, padel has surely built a solid following.

Whilst Argentina and Spain remain the primary padel nations, other countries in South America, Europe, and Asia have been witnessing a surge of interest in the sport. Particularly in Asia – where padel was introduced first in Japan, in 2013, then in Singapore the following year – the number of courts is constantly ticking up. In the past five years or so, nations like Thailand, UAE, China, Qatar, and India have seen the emergence of padel clubs and tournaments, which have consequently helped spread the word and consolidate the market.

In Europe, one of the most notable and thriving hubs of padel, the sport has established a strong foothold. Since 2017, tennis federations of almost every EU country have integrated padel into their framework, providing steadfast consultation and setting up development plans to further the growth of the sport. These schemes focus on increasing the number of padel courts, optimising padel learning programmes and coach certifications, improving infrastructure to make the sport more accessible, expanding the network of partnerships and sponsors, and raising awareness of the sport through events.

Spain – a country with roughly 4 million active players,

and where about 25% of all padel courts are situated at tennis clubs – is a great example of the dynamics between tennis and padel. Indeed, the national padel fever began at tennis venues. However, the increasing demand over the past decade has incited enthusiasts and business people to set up venues particularly for the practice of padel. This initiative has also done much to facilitate the dissemination of the sport across the country, not only through exposure but also for the fact that with so many padel courts all around, booking prices have decreased. Nevertheless, such a phenomenon highlights the fact that for growth to be sustainable and facilities to thrive, organisation and watertight business models are needed. The current parameter for a financially feasible padel club in Spain is a minimum of six courts, and it wouldn't be far-fetched to extend these projections to other European nations with an emerging padel scene.

Among the up-and-coming padel nations, Sweden is probably the leader when it comes to the speed and scale of growth. This surge is both due to the "stickiness" of the trend and the increasing number of enthusiasts, as well as the strategic way developments are being carried out. Entrepreneurs aware of the business potential are building courts and founding clubs, often reaching out to celebrities to promote them. As a reaction, Stockholm has recently welcomed an indoor venue with 20 padel courts. Still, making sure the domestic industry grows sustainably is very much a joint effort, so the solidification and dissemination of padel in Sweden will also come down to how the Swedish Padel Federation manages this abrupt maturation.

Meanwhile, European nations such as France and Italy have also witnessed tremendous growth. The number of courts has gone from less than 100 to almost a thousand in just five years. Again, a lot of this growth has been influenced by the fact that tennis federations in these countries (as well as in 19 other European nations) now oversee padel-related matters. This newly founded structure of governance has consequently supported and promoted the practice of padel, enticing several tennis facilities to build padel courts and cross-pollinating cultures and profits.

For tennis federations, establishing a harmonious relationship with padel means a multifaceted backup – one that can boost membership. Here is a sport that shares many of tennis' qualities, but which provides a more inclusive – and perhaps more fun – alternative to racquet sports' aficionados. In light of this, tennis clubs are tapping into the growing popularity and expanded demographics of padel to solve some of their structural and financial challenges. In other words, more padel courts in tennis facilities entice more padel players to join the clubs, consequently enhancing the potential for more people to take up tennis whilst setting up a new revenue stream for the club itself.

In the UK, another budding padel nation, the sport has been incorporated into the Lawn Tennis Association (LTA). Although the UK hasn't yet been a boom such as that of Sweden, having a well-structured governing body stimulating and sponsoring developments will surely spur popularity in the coming years. Among other initiatives, the LTA currently has a loan scheme in place aimed at padel projects. Promotions like this will help the country achieve its goal of 400 courts by 2023, placing the UK padel scene shoulder to shoulder with neighbours like Belgium and the Netherlands.

Besides enhancing expansion, another important milestone – and indeed a goal that has been set for padel as a sport – is making it to the Olympic Games. This is no easy feat, however. To obtain Olympic status, a sport has to meet a range of criteria, namely having a recognised international federation by the ARISF (Association of IOC Recognised International Sports Federations); an elite-level competition series; and registered male players on at least four continents and female players on at least three continents. Padel has already reached many of these standards: it has the World Padel Tour, registered federations with male and female players on six continents, and was acknowledged as an international sport by the International Olympic Committee in 2019. However, it is yet to reach the minimum per-country requirement. There are currently 40 national federations representing female players, but in the men's category, the number of national federations hasn't made the threshold of 75. This is the last step before padel is eligible to apply for the Olympics entry list. Then, it will be included in the official review session conducted by the IOC during the year following the Olympic Games. If it gets a thumbs up, padel will have made it to the Olympics.

As it stands, however, padel is in a good, positive place – it is ascending. The journey is ongoing, but steps are continuously taking the sport forward. With or without an Olympic status, the fact that padel is such a fun, social, accessible (both financially, physically, as well as age and gender-wise), and rewarding sport makes it easy for more followers to jump on the bandwagon. Add to that a growing market with investment and sponsorship opportunities and increasing media coverage of the World Padel Tour, and you have the solid foundation for a trend that is here to stay.